The Philosopher's
Stone
in the Gospels and in Alchemy

Translated from the French
Original title: « LA PIERRE PHILOSOPHALE
des Évangiles aux traités alchimiques »

Original edition:
© 2003, Éditions Prosveta S.A., ISBN 978-2-85566-876-5

Prosveta S.A – B.P.12 – 83601 Fréjus CEDEX (France)
ISSN 0763-2738
ISBN 978-2-85566-950-2

Omraam Mikhaël Aïvanhov

The Philosopher's Stone

in the Gospels and in Alchemy

Izvor Collection – No. 241

PROSVETA

Readers are asked to note that Omraam Mikhaël Aïvanhov's teaching was exclusively oral. This volume includes passages from several different lectures all dealing with the same theme.

TABLE OF CONTENTS

Chapter One

ON THE INTERPRETATION
OF THE SCRIPTURES

I

'The Letter Kills, but the Spirit Gives Life'

You have noticed that when I want to clarify an important point for you about the spiritual life, I often refer to the Bible, especially the Gospels. When I do so, however, I am fully aware that some of you are thinking, 'But why does he attach so much importance to what's written in these wretched Gospels, when it's been shown time and again that they've been tampered with, doctored and mutilated and are even contradictory? Why does he continue to base his teaching on these texts?' This kind of thinking proves you haven't understood me properly. I don't attach absolute value to the letter of the Gospels, but I use them as a starting point for bringing to light the eternal truths taught by Jesus.

Here is an image. A starry sky is one of the greatest wonders in nature, but there are different ways of looking at the stars. You can take along a map of the heavens and an astronomy book that will reveal in detail everything known about the stars and planets: their names, the distances between them, what they are each made of, how they are born, how they live and die, the physical laws governing the solar system, and so on. This is all certainly very useful and interesting for our understanding of the universe, but what does it contribute to our soul and spirit?

I have read books on astronomy, I have listened to astronomers present their research, and often I have been very impressed. But how different this is from the experience I have had of contemplating a starry sky, with no desire other than to dissolve in its immensity! A sense of peace stole over me little by little, lifting me higher; my only wish was to tear myself from the earth, to go far into space and make contact with the spiritual entities that manifest physically as stars. Once projected into these regions, I felt nothing was more important than to unite with the cosmic Spirit and allow it to penetrate me, to bring me to a true understanding of things, an understanding which permeated my every cell.[1]

When we are faced with the immensity and splendour of the heavens, we sometimes feel lost. But losing ourselves in contemplation of the sky is not a goal; we must go further, for the starry sky is also a book, one that speaks not just to our intellect. The knowledge it imparts to us is imprinted within us and can transform our lives. This is true knowledge: we are illumined by a light that surpasses us, a light that orientates our thoughts, our feelings and our actions.

Astronomers observe the night sky, but most of them confine themselves to its material reality.

Unaware that there are intelligent beings inhabiting and working on these celestial bodies, they reduce everything to mechanical laws, so their soul and spirit gain little from their studies. They are like mountaineers whose only goal in scaling a summit is athletic achievement or the study of rocks or atmospheric variations. They forget to look at the mountain and commune with its beauty, its purity and its power.

Contemplating a starry sky, like climbing a mountain, should give human beings the solution to all their problems, because it opens the doors to the heavens within them. Those who become accustomed to looking at the stars with love – who meditate on cosmic harmony, on these lights that have come such a great distance in time and space – travel in thought through the spiritual realms that also lie within themselves. Understand that this is how I read the sacred books, in particular the Bible: as if I were standing before a sky whose stars illuminate and penetrate my whole life.

The Bible has played an enormous role in the formation of the human spirit. It has been read and reread. It has been translated into all the languages of the world, and it is even said that more copies of this book have been printed than of any other. Many people who own a Bible either read it very little or not at all but keep it as a sort of talisman. And many who do read it confess they don't really understand these texts and sometimes feel discouraged.

Over the centuries, Christians have simply read the Bible without questioning. In some homes there were no other books. Many people have actually learned to read using the Bible and have made it their daily sustenance. But now this text is becoming more and more foreign to current ways of thinking. So many people – Catholic, Protestant and Orthodox – have confided to me that, in spite of their best efforts, reading the Bible does little for them. So what did readers in the old days understand that today's men and women no longer do?

Some say we understand the Bible by reading and re-reading it, and we must also prepare for this reading with prayer and fasting. Others advocate studying the written commentaries. This advice certainly has something to recommend it, but it's not where the real answer lies. And, in many cases, commentators who have set out to study the Bible from a scientific perspective have even minimized its value. Their analyses have mostly brought to light errors in transcription, omissions and contradictions, and instead of finding inspiration and enlightenment they have only amassed material for endless discussion and controversy. Scientific methods are always useful, of course, but their efficacy is uneven, depending on the area of study. The mysteries of the soul escape them, and they grasp only an infinitesimal part of reality.

It is certainly interesting to think about when a certain part of the Old or New Testament may have been written, whether there was one author or several, and to examine the vocabulary and compare it to that of related languages. But this approach, which consists of analysing, digging and dissecting, often leaves nothing more than dust and ashes in its wake. Understanding the sacred books, whether it's the Vedas, the Zend-Avesta or the Koran, requires discipline of a different kind.

The first rule is to put yourself in a receptive state, to allow the images and sensations evoked by your reading to work on your subconscious. In this way, the more you read the Bible, the more you will feel a clarity developing in you. Otherwise, you will only succeed in moving further from the meaning. Eventually you will even adopt an attitude of indifference and scepticism, as if it all merited no more than the slightest curiosity. You will tell yourself it's always interesting to discover what the human brain is capable of, since those who invented God, the soul, the spirit and other worlds have demonstrated such originality and imagination! But with an attitude like that, you will not nourish your inner life.

Everything that is said in the sacred books is correct, not according to the criteria of the intellect perhaps, which always keeps to the letter of the text, but correct where the soul and spirit are concerned. This is the meaning of St. Paul's words in his *Second Letter to the Corinthians: 'The letter kills, but the Spirit gives life.'*

The truths expressed in the Bible have been lived by exceptional souls. If we are to understand these

truths, we must strive to follow these souls to the
realms they themselves managed to reach, in other
words to see things as they saw them. Are we able
to interpret the parables of Jesus any better simply
because we've studied the grammar of an ancient
language, the history of a people or the archaeology?
No, if we are to interpret his parables, a different kind
of science is needed, the science of symbols, which
can only be acquired by exercising the faculties of
the soul and spirit.

We cannot understand the sacred texts unless our
being can vibrate at the same wavelength as those
who wrote them. Their language, their true language,
remains foreign to us. We must feel what they felt,
live what they lived; in other words, we must rise to
their level of consciousness. That's when the light
will truly shine out![2]

But this higher level of consciousness can only
be achieved if we improve our way of life, if we
become more mindful and respectful of the laws
of the spiritual world. So many people believe they
can project themselves onto higher planes without
changing anything in the way they live and think!
No, they can indulge all they like in all kinds of wild
imaginings, but they will never get beyond the 'letter'
and will fail to understand.

It is thanks to their life of discipline that the
patriarchs and prophets, who were initiates, were
able to elevate themselves to the divine world.
We too must adopt a disciplined life, if we are to
rise as they did to the place where they had their

revelations, for there is no other way. So if you want to read the Bible, begin by asking yourself what you need to improve in your life, and don't worry about understanding everything immediately. There are so many difficult texts! *Genesis,* for example, or the book of *Revelations...* But read without troubling yourself, and try to elevate yourself through thought, by praying to the Holy Spirit to come and bring you its light.

On several occasions I have read you the passage from the *Gospel According to John* known as the Sacerdotal Prayer: *'Father, the hour has come; glorify your Son so that the Son may glorify you, since you have given him authority over all flesh, to give eternal life to all whom you have given him.'* Perhaps this passage can't be understood intellectually, but because it comes from the soul and spirit of Christ it speaks to our own soul and spirit and exercises its power over them. Once these words have touched our soul and spirit, our entire being, including our physical body, feels their vibrations. *'I have made your name known to those whom you gave me from the world. They were yours, and you gave them to me, and they have kept your word... The glory that you have given me I have given them, so that they may be one, as we are one, I in them and you in me, that they may become completely one, so that the world may know that you have sent me and have loved them even as you have loved me. Father, I desire that those also, whom you have given me, may be with me where I am, to see my glory, which you have given me because you loved me before the foundation of the world.'*

Yes, when these vibrations from the world of the soul and spirit are felt in our whole being, something that has lain dormant in us awakens and is set in motion. The Biblical texts, often criticized by scholars for their style, are like currents of energy which have the power to reawaken souls, to satisfy their hunger and heal them. The Sacerdotal Prayer is one of the most authentic, true and profound passages we can read. And too bad for those who limit themselves to a critical analysis of it!

During the last supper with his disciples, Jesus said, *'... Now I am going to him who sent me... I still have many things to say to you, but you cannot bear them now. When the Spirit of Truth comes, he will guide you into all the truth.'*[3] With these words, Jesus was drawing his disciples' attention to the essential role of the spirit. Yes, the spirit, not the letter! So immerse yourself in the words of the Gospels, meditate on them, exalting their essence within you and linking yourself with the entities of heaven. The day you succeed in experiencing these great truths as living, active realities within you, your entire inner being will be purified, enlightened and regenerated by them.

Notes
1. See *The Path of Silence,* Izvor 229, chap. 13: 'The revelations of a starry sky'.

2. See *'Et il me montra un fleuve d'eau de la vie'*, Part VIII, chap. 3: 'L'ascension des montagnes spirituelles'.
3. See *Truth, Fruit of Wisdom and Love*, Izvor 234, chap. 7: 'The blue ray of truth'.

II

The Word of God

Without the light of initiatic Science, a correct interpretation of the Bible is impossible. We approach this Science through study, of course, through our reading and the teachings of a sage or master. But we acquire what is essential through a discipline based on the development of our spiritual organs, for when we develop these organs we acquire the ability to project ourselves into other regions of space to investigate them.[1] These are the experiences recounted by St. John in the book of *Revelations* and by St. Paul in his *Second Letter to the Corinthians*. St. John writes: *'I, John... was in the spirit on the Lord's day, and I heard behind me a loud voice like a trumpet saying, "Write in a book what you see..."'* And St. Paul: *'I know a person in Christ who fourteen years ago was caught up to the third heaven – whether in the body or out of the body I do not know, God knows. And I know that this person was caught up into Paradise – whether in the body or out of the body I do not know,*

*God knows – and heard things that cannot be told,
that no mortal is permitted to repeat.'*

Only such experiences can grant us access to
the reality of the divine world. Aside from these, the
books we seek out to read will give us a glimpse,
an orientation, but this is not enough. In order to
learn, we must then go elsewhere to be instructed, to
live something else. This journey elsewhere, which
mystics call ecstasy, occurs when one's being is
projected out of one's body. I too have had to pass
through these experiences in order to know what I
know now; I haven't found it in books. I have found
things mentioned, confirmed and verified in books,
but I have made the discoveries themselves far, far
away from my body.

And why is it necessary to project oneself like
this into higher worlds? Because it is only from above
that we see things correctly. From below, we see only
a scattered, fragmented reality. And so long as we
do not see an order, a structure, in other words the
connections which unify all elements and all levels
of creation, we cannot correctly interpret texts which
were inspired by a vision of divine unity.

Sacred books are the transposition into words
of experiences certain people have had in the world
above, a world different from the one we perceive
with our five senses. If we are to understand these
beings, if we are to know their thinking, we too must
go and explore on high, to see what they saw and
feel what they felt.[2] But where are those who will
set out on this ascent with a firm resolve to reach the

summit? People make an effort for a few days and then, disappointed that they haven't achieved quick results, give up; they're content to study the books of a few monks, philosophers or scientists. This is easier, of course, but only seems to be, since the answers they find there are often so contradictory!

Let's just take philosophical works... So many philosophers invent systems which only take into account their own vision of the world! This vision, which is necessarily limited, reflects their spiritual, psychological, intellectual, even physical shortcomings. And that's not to mention those who attempt to come up with new theories, in their quest to cultivate originality. There are as many philosophies as there are philosophers! The truth is that there is only one system which explains the universe, in other words only one system which renders an account of the Creator, the creation and its creatures, and each of us must try to discover for ourselves the fundamentals of this system. The fact that we all express the results of this search according to our own temperament, our own character and sensibility, in other words in our own 'voice', is perfectly normal.

Singers who have to perform a musical piece can only do so with their own voice, and through their voice they express who they are in the deepest sense. But they must respect the score; they are not at liberty to sing notes other than those written. In the same way, philosophers have no right to sing words other than those inscribed in the great book of life; they only have the right to sing them with their own throat. This is what I myself have endeavoured to do ever since I discovered the light of initiatic Science. Now that I have found the one true philosophy, the one true science, the one true religion – and the three are really only one – I try to adhere to it without asking whether it corresponds to my tastes or inclinations.

Of course, there are a number of rich and profound books that can set us on the path, but true knowledge – that which becomes flesh and bone in us – is only acquired when we succeed in elevating ourselves to the divine world, where all things have their origin. The great founders of religions received their inspiration from on high. According to tradition, it was the archangels who instructed them: Moses is said to have been instructed by Metatron, Mohammed by the archangel Gabriel, and so on. Which is another way of saying true knowledge comes from on high and that's where we must look for it. The same truths are revealed to everyone capable of ascending to the higher planes of consciousness. The form and expression they take will differ, but the principles are the same.

You believe that libraries exist only on earth – your own library, those of your acquaintances, or the public libraries where you can go to read or borrow books. No, you must understand there are other libraries with other books you can also consult. These books represent all the records stored in the universe and within the human being, since everything, yes, everything, down to the most minor event and the least word, is recorded.

How many times have I explained to you that the phenomena of the physical world can shed light for us on the realities of the psychic and spiritual worlds! You listen to the radio, you watch television; often these programmes have been pre-recorded, or they are recorded at the time of broadcast. Every radio and television company, therefore, owns archives, which can be consulted at any time, to reveal what was actually said or shown.

Human beings have shown great ingenuity in perfecting instruments capable of recording images and sounds, but nature herself has been making recordings since the beginning of time! And the reason these recordings are possible is because matter is not inert and unresponsive. Not only is matter sentient, it is also endowed with memory. Every event that occurs leaves traces in the deep layers of matter; nothing happens that is not recorded, and nothing disappears. It is simply that human beings have not yet developed the means of reading or hearing these recordings.

No, human beings do not know themselves; they have no idea of the faculties the Creator has put at their disposal. Nor do they know that they represent a microcosm, a reflection of the universal macrocosm, and as such are repositories of the whole of cosmic memory. In the subtle and imponderable substance that makes up the quintessence of our being, there is room enough for the entire universe. For, given the structure of matter, the infinite diversity of the phenomena that occur can be reduced to an infinitesimal point.

The most distant events in the cosmos, the upheavals of lost worlds and news from the whole world all make their way to us, where they are recorded by our inner instruments. Obviously, this information remains in our subconscious and only rarely reaches our awareness. We can compare this to what happens in the case of radio waves. The very existence of radios demonstrates that there is a mass of information circulating throughout space; we do not consciously detect these waves, but instruments designed for the purpose allow us to capture them.

At this very moment, countless waves are passing through space, coming from all parts of the earth as well as other planets and constellations. These waves intersect and become entangled without obliterating each other, each able to be picked up by an instrument tuned to its frequency. They pass through us as well, but we do not feel them. And just as well! If, even for a moment, our brain began to record everything happening in the universe, it would be intolerable!

Here is another example. Every day head librarians receive not only books but newspapers, magazines and reviews of all kinds, but they don't take on the task of reading them all: they would soon be mentally exhausted, and a twenty-four hour day wouldn't be long enough. It is the employees responsible for different departments who take charge of putting them on the shelves, and if the librarian needs to consult a document, he or she sends for it. Like the librarian, we too are repositories for all the information that has ever existed or is now coming to light. When we want to reflect on certain subjects so as to understand them more deeply, we can ask to be provided with whatever documents we need.

When I explained the parable of the dishonest manager[3] to you, I showed you that, given the text's apparent contradictions, its meaning cannot be revealed to us if we simply work as scholars do. But if we elevate ourselves to the level of the cosmic library, we will be able to fill in the gaps in the Gospel text. Only on high can all disciples of the divine school hope to read the great Book from which Jesus drew his knowledge. But unlike the libraries on earth, this one is not open to everyone; it is guarded by very powerful entities, which only allow access to those who have prepared for a very long time, and it is not easy to hoist oneself up to that level!

But it is also true that there is a library we can gain access to every day, for it is found within us. You may say, 'Then why don't we consult it more often?' To use an analogy: the books found here are written in such minuscule characters you have to enlarge them with the help of a strong magnifying glass, and because humans don't possess this magnifying glass to enlarge the characters, they give up trying to read them. So you must begin by obtaining the magnifying glass that will enable you to read all the documents in your inner library. Yes, the only problem is the size of the images. Every request made to this library is granted. No matter what your question, you receive an answer, but because the images delivered to you are so minute you think you have received nothing.

For the entire universe to be represented in man, it must have been reduced by billions of times. So it's natural that we can't see these images, let alone decipher them, without installing a magnifying glass as well as a projector. Perhaps you have held up a strip of film and noticed how small and blurred the images are; even against the light you can scarcely distinguish any forms. But once they have been projected onto a screen, the enlarged images become clear and precise.

So in order to have images of the right size, you need a projector. 'But where can I find one?' you will ask. In your consciousness.[4] The camera, however, is found in the subconscious, where everything is recorded automatically. But in order for you to acquire the projector to decipher the documents in your own library, it is necessary for you to have initiatic knowledge and a discipline. Only by means of this knowledge and this discipline can you develop in your consciousness the necessary elements for interpreting the responses you receive.

Perhaps you find it odd that I'm referring to radio and the cinema in the context of the knowledge and interpretation of sacred texts, but they are the clearest explanations I can give you. And, as I have already shown you several times, progress in science and technology, far from attacking religion and spirituality, actually gives us better ways to understand the principles on which they are founded. This is why, if the Bible and all the sacred books were to disappear, we could recreate them, because they have their origins in the one true book, the book of life, in other words the universe and human beings themselves, the repositories for the word of God.

The divine word transmitted by the sacred texts is obviously not a word in the usual sense of the term. Whatever some may think, God has never addressed himself to human beings in a human language to reveal himself to them or give them instructions. It is they who read and hear the word of God in nature and in themselves, for the divine Word, the primordial light, forms the substance of everything that exists. But people have not yet understood the meaning of the third verse of *Genesis: 'God said, "Let there be light!"'*, nor its echo in the first verse of the *Gospel According to John: 'In the beginning was the Word.'*[5] The human word is only a very remote and faint expression of the divine word, of this divine Word. And because we use 'word' for both, this leads to a great deal of confusion.

It is said that God spoke to the initiates, to the hierophants and prophets. In reality, God has been speaking and continues to speak through all of creation and in the hearts of men and women themselves. So it is not correct to say that he spoke exclusively to this or that person; it would be fairer to say that some people have heard him better than others. And we should also add that what they have heard and reported has been inevitably determined by the situation, problems and mentality of their times. Where the great principles are concerned, they have all said the same thing, but when we go into the details we realize that prescriptions which were undoubtedly acceptable and perhaps even necessary some centuries ago, and which represented real progress since they responded to particular needs, are today no longer acceptable.

All sacred books are incomplete or imperfect, and often we don't even know who wrote and transmitted them or under what conditions. And there have been so many exceptional beings, sages, mystics and poets who have also been able to hear and read the divine word! Many of them have written nothing, or, if they have written, their works have been lost. Or, if they have not been lost, tradition doesn't present them as sacred books, even though they too contain essential revelations concerning the world of the soul and spirit and its inhabitants.

The time has come for believers of all religions to stop attacking each other, to stop brandishing their sacred books as the only repositories of the word of God, for this is wrong. Yes, wrong and ridiculous. True faith gains nothing by these arguments. Religions have depicted the Lord in a way that was no doubt good in an epoch when the vast majority of human beings were not very developed mentally. Now that their capacity for understanding is more refined, why continue to tell them that it is God himself who spoke to the prophets and that the so-called sacred texts contain only eternal truths?

Let's be very clear about this. All sacred books are as yet only a few fragments, a few incomplete and imperfect copies of the only book truly written by God: the universe, with the human being created in the image of the universe. Some will shout 'sacrilege' or 'heresy'. Well, let them shout what they like. For my part, I know that heaven is listening to me and agrees with me. It is only the ignorant who will be indignant, since they do not know how the Creator conceived of the universe or of humankind.

Even if they were inspired by heaven – and they certainly were – the sacred books do not contain only indisputable and definitive truths. And we are well aware that the versions we know today have undergone all sorts of alterations. For instance, the five books of the *Pentateuch* attributed to Moses were in fact laid down in their present form several centuries after him, under the authority of Esdras. As for the Old Testament itself, Jews, Catholics, Protestants and Orthodox Christians do not even agree on how many books it contains. And as for the Gospels, it is obvious that the four short works, which say more or less the same thing, cannot represent the totality of Jesus' teaching.

There is so much that could be said about how the sacred books were compiled and disseminated! But I am no historian, and to enter into all these details doesn't interest me. I know what I know, and that is enough for me. And what do I know? That even though the sacred books are neither definitive nor complete as they stand, if we learn how to read them they will show us all the path to God. A true initiate will never present a sacred book as the definitive book, not even the Bible, though many consider it to be *the* book *par excellence,* since the word 'bible' means 'book'. In every sacred book, something could be corrected, taken out or added.

Those who manage to rise to an understanding of God's works can rediscover the quintessence of all the sacred books, for the truths they contain are inscribed in the life of the universe and in our own life. God himself is inaccessible, unfathomable and beyond all understanding, but he has placed within us and in his created universe all the elements that allow us to come close to him and decipher some of his messages. And which of these messages is the most essential? Light, since it was through light that he manifested himself at the creation of the world, when he said, *'Let there be light!'* Therefore, if we want to hear God 'speak' to us, we must look to the light, for it is through light that he addresses all his creatures.[6]

Notes
1. See *Man's Subtle Bodies and Centres,* Izvor 219.
2. See *Life and Work in an Initiatic School,* CW 30, chap 3: 'Training for the Divine', part V.
3. See *'You are Gods',* part II, chap. 2: 'No one can serve two masters'.

4. See *'Et il me montra un fleuve d'eau de la vie'*, part VI, chap. 1: 'L'écran de la conscience'.
5. See *'Cherchez le Royaume de Dieu et sa Justice'*, part II: 'Sur la terre comme au ciel', 1 and 2.
6. See *Light is a Living Spirit*, Izvor 212, chap. 5: 'Working with light'.

Chapter Two

'IT IS NOT WHAT GOES
INTO THE MOUTH
THAT DEFILES A PERSON…'

Someone who had read the chapter on vegetarianism[1] in one of my books on nutrition asked me the following question: 'Is it so important not to eat meat? Jesus says in a passage in the Gospels that it's not what goes into the mouth that defiles a human being but what comes out of it.' It's true, Jesus did say this, but from what this person said next I saw that she had not really understood the meaning of Jesus' words. For this reason, I would like to go back to this passage and explain what it means.

Addressing the crowd that was following him, Jesus said, *'Listen and understand: it is not what goes into the mouth that defiles a person, but it is what comes out of the mouth that defiles.'* After Jesus had spoken these words, his disciples came to him to report that the Pharisees had been scandalized by what he had said. Then Peter said to him, *'Explain this parable to us.'* And Jesus replied, *'Are you also still without understanding? Do you not see that whatever goes into the mouth enters the stomach,*

*and goes out into the sewer? But what comes out of
the mouth proceeds from the heart, and this is what
defiles.'*

What goes into our mouth? Food primarily,
and unless there are digestive problems this food
doesn't come back out the same way. It is mainly
words that come out of our mouth. But can it be
said that food never defiles us? If it is not well
washed or has been polluted by toxic products,
it can make us ill. But the word 'defile' has more
to do with the moral realm. Certain foods, certain
substances can influence our moral life due to
the effects they produce: meat, alcohol and drugs
all have consequences to different degrees on a
person's psychic life and, therefore, on their moral
life. This is why from their inception most religions
have imposed very strict rules concerning food and
drink. There were certainly reasons for these rules,
but on the other hand many of those who respected
them had no scruples when it came to transgressing
the basic principles of justice, honesty or kindness.
This is a reproach Jesus levelled at the Pharisees,
and it is one that would still apply today to some of
the faithful of other religions.

*'But what comes out of the mouth proceeds
from the heart, and this is what defiles.'* In order
to understand Jesus' words, we must refer to what
initiatic Science reveals to us about the different
bodies that constitute the human being: physical,
astral, mental, causal, buddhic and atmic.

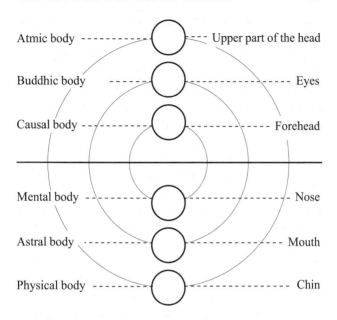

The astral body is the seat of the emotions, of feelings and desires, and is therefore represented in us by what we call the heart. Now remember what I explained to you in the lecture entitled 'What the human face reveals'.[2] In it I showed you the relationships that exist between the forehead and the spirit, between the eyes and the soul, between the nose and the intellect, and between the mouth and the heart. The mouth expresses what comes from the heart, from the astral body.

This then is the meaning of Jesus' words: what comes out of the mouth comes from the heart, and it is this that defiles humans if they have not learned to

purify their astral body. The mouth that is meant here
is obviously the astral mouth. Nothing physical comes
out of our physical mouth, since it only swallows
and absorbs. In contrast, many things come out of
our astral mouth: feelings, emotions and desires are
expressed through it, and if they are inspired by our
lower nature we become defiled. Before we defile
others, we defile ourselves.

In fact, there is a very strong connection between
the two mouths, the physical and the astral. If
you satisfy the physical mouth, the astral mouth
immediately expresses its pleasure and contentment
through a look, a smile, a word. People are well
aware of this, which is why they give so much
attention to the choice and preparation of food when
they invite their relatives and friends. By offering
them a delicious meal that's pleasing to their physical
mouth, they reckon they will also satisfy the astral
mouth. Conversely, people who are malnourished,
because they indiscriminately swallow whatever's to
hand, or because they have nothing else to eat, will
not be able to express much goodness through their
astral mouth, that is to say through their heart. So
Jesus' words are not to be taken literally, and though
we should not give too much importance to dietary
prescriptions, it is not good to go too far the other
way either, neglecting certain standards of hygiene.
Jesus did not recommend eating anything anyhow.

What enters us passes through the physical
mouth, and what comes out passes through the astral

mouth. But is it really true that nothing enters our astral mouth? No, for in the same way that we feel and express emotions and desires, we also receive the emotions and desires felt and expressed by others. And sometimes these feelings and desires are truly toxic products, poisons, which can do us a great deal of harm. It is possible to neutralize these by transforming them, but it is only when you have done a great deal of work on yourself that you can bear to see and hear all the madness and criminality that humans are capable of, without being poisoned or destroyed by it. Only the initiates, the great masters, know how to rid such 'foods' of their poison and capacity to do harm and then express only noble and generous feelings through their astral mouth. So Jesus' words are addressed to neither the weak nor the ignorant.

Every day you yourself are exposed to the influences and stresses of the outside world. These are foods you absorb. But if a look, a word, a gesture or an action can rob you of your faith, love and light, so that you become unclean, this too means that you do not know how to nourish yourself: you should have selected your foods more carefully or kept your mouth shut, symbolically speaking. Why did you open it to these foods? If you don't then know how to transform them, you shouldn't accept them.

You may say, 'But how can we avoid being upset and wounded by certain unkind remarks or attitudes?' On the physical plane, of course, it's impossible, but Jesus' words do not actually concern the physical plane. The astral mouth within us is fully capable of rejecting such food, and since it then does no damage to our integrity or our dignity as sons or daughters of God we do not feel belittled or wounded. It is possible for insults, slander or any other darkness to enter a person's astral mouth without ever tainting him or her. Only what comes from within yourself can defile you. You are responsible for nothing else. For the sage and the initiate, then, Jesus' words are entirely true.

In centuries past, a man or woman's honour was based above all on social values, that is to say on external values. A word or gesture that offended a nobleman's honour immediately required him to fight a duel, to defend his reputation or that of his family in the eyes of society and future generations. Everything that affected human beings, that 'entered their mouth', tainted them. They had to 'wash their honour clean', and endless tragedies arose out of next to nothing. Those who would not retaliate were considered despicable and cowardly; they lost the esteem of others and were rejected by them. French literature of the seventeenth century, as you know, is full of stories of this kind.

There is no doubt that this custom and way of seeing things required men to behave with courage. But from the moral and spiritual viewpoint, this concept of honour is wrong, deplorable and stupid, for instead of developing real nobility and courage it was used only to save face, to maintain social prestige, which is really worth very little. In order to maintain their prestige in the eyes of men, they diminished themselves a thousandfold in the eyes of God.

True nobility consists in seeking more intelligent solutions, through recourse to conciliation. But this requires an entire inner work first: the offended party must understand that there is no malice or accusation that can diminish them in the eyes of God. If they are innocent, accusations and slander make no difference to the way they are seen by the angels and by God himself.

Some people are unable to tolerate a small glass of wine; they immediately get drunk and say all sorts of foolish things. And in the same way, there are people who lose their head over the slightest thing that annoys them. In contrast, truly spiritual people can drink all the intoxicating liquor the astral plane sends them and still maintain a clear gaze, lucid thought and a straight and steady gait.

Jesus was not unaware of the fact that some foods can defile us, but he also knew that we have the capacity to resist them. Every day we are presented with temptations offered to us like so many foods. To be tempted is to receive an influence. And what is an influence? It is a current which attempts to enter us and, therefore, a kind of food. It is not always possible to withstand the irruption of these currents, but once they have been introduced we must try our hardest to transform them. If we succumb, if we give in to an act of weakness, our inner judge registers that we haven't been able to assimilate these substances, and they will reappear in one way or another in the form of impurities, of psychological or even physical disorders.

If you don't allow harmful 'foods' in, there will be no risk of their going back out again, so you must take care not to let them in. But as you cannot always manage to do this, once they have gained entry you must make every effort to transform them so they can be assimilated.

In ancient times there lived a king called Mithradates who, from fear of being poisoned by people in his entourage, sought to immunize himself by taking progressively larger doses of poison. This proved very successful: having lost a battle and not wanting to be captured alive by his enemies, he swallowed all sorts of poison, but to no avail, and in the end he had to ask one of his soldiers to stab him to death. It is true that you can become physically invulnerable to the effects of poisons. Mithradates isn't the only one to have done so, but is it that necessary? It's unlikely that any of you runs the risk of being poisoned. Every day, however, each of you is exposed to all sorts of psychic poisons, and if you do not know how to react to them, you will succumb.

Disciples of an initiatic school must learn to digest all the poisons ignorant or malicious people can pour for them on the astral plane. These are the poisons Jesus was speaking of when he said, *'Blessed are you when people revile you and persecute you and utter all kinds of evil against you falsely.'* So whatever happens, rejoice, and heaven will rejoice in you, because you will have passed the test.

At some time or another, everyone is slandered and besmirched. True disciples of Christ are those who know how to neutralize the filth they receive without uttering a word against God or other people. And if they do happen to let words of irritation, outrage or revenge slip out, at the very least they have to take stock and tell themselves, 'I must never forget that it's what leaves my mouth that defiles me... I was given substances I didn't know how to use, but in future I will try to transform my anger and impatience into gentleness, love and kindness.' Like a good cook, the disciple must learn the art of transformation and make good use of everything on offer to prepare the best dishes. Yes, even cooking has something to teach us here!

And look at trees: when we give them manure, they say, 'We are well aware that what goes into our mouths cannot defile us.' So they go to work, knowing the secret of how to bring about transformations, and what they give back to us are fruits as beautiful, fragrant and delectable as the manure they received was ugly, foul-smelling and repulsive. But how do human beings tend to act? They receive a little splash and send back a whole bucket of filth! If they understood Christ's commandments, they would make every effort when they receive venom to give honey in return.

So how should you respond when a gesture, a word or a look has provoked embarrassment, anger

or some other negative state in you? First of all, stop;
pause for a moment, for if you allow yourself to be
carried away by your instinctive reactions, you risk
causing more harm than was done to you. Anger is
an irruption of a brute force, which is not necessarily
a bad thing; it can even be beneficial for yourself and
others, so long as you know how to master it and
direct it. And in order to master it, you must first lay
down the weapons that this instinctive reaction has
suddenly placed at your disposal. First of all, then,
you must stop, be quiet and think, for reason is the
only branch or rock you can hold on to if you are not
to be swept along and tossed about in the torrential
waters. The fact that you have stopped proves that
you know what to hold on to, that you haven't been
carried away by the torrent's wild currents.

But once you have stopped, how do you put right
the turmoil you feel? By taking a deep breath, by
making a few harmonious, rhythmical movements
with your legs, arms and head. Know that even if
you are bound hand and foot, just one free finger will
enable you to restore balance, peace and harmony in
yourself. You can also visualize writing magic words
in letters of light: peace, wisdom, love, beauty…
These very simple methods produce remarkable
results; again, you need to maintain enough lucidity
and self-control to think of using them.

*'What comes out of the mouth proceeds from the
heart…'* Actually, you could say the mouth Jesus is
speaking of stands for the different mouths of our

psychic being – not only of the heart, but also of our
intellect and will. So the word 'mouth' symbolizes the
whole of our activity. Just as our heart is the mouth
through which our feelings pass, so our intellect is
the mouth through which our thoughts are expressed
and our will the mouth that will produce action. It is
worth meditating on what the mouth is capable of: it
builds or destroys, it soils or purifies, it imprisons or
sets free, it hangs a man or plucks him from the jaws
of death. This is yet another meaning of the first verse
of the *Gospel According to John: 'In the beginning
was the Word...'* How many happy and unhappy
events start with the mouth![3]

In the book of *Genesis,* it is said that after Adam
and Eve had eaten the forbidden fruit, they hid from
the Lord, who was walking in the garden in the
evening breeze. God called to Adam, *"Where are
you?"* and then a whole conversation ensued. Adam
replied, *'"I heard the sound of you in the garden, and
I was afraid, because I was naked; and I hid myself."
He said, "Who told you that you were naked? Have
you eaten from the tree of which I commanded you
not to eat?" The man said, "The woman whom you
gave to be with me, she gave me fruit from the tree,
and I ate." Then the Lord God said to the woman,
"What is this that you have done?" The woman said,
"The serpent tricked me, and I ate."'* [4]

One tradition recounts that the fruit Adam and
Eve ate was an apple, another that it was a fig... It
doesn't matter; the point is that this passage refers
to the same subject as Jesus' teaching, namely, food.

The snake, which is a personification of evil, tempts
Eve by suggesting that she eat the forbidden fruit,
and Eve then proposes the same to Adam. When God
asks them what has happened, Adam blames Eve,
and Eve blames the serpent. Of course, placing the
blame for their mistakes on a tempter – or temptress –
doesn't excuse them. If we have acted badly, we are
guilty. We should simply not succumb, not 'eat',
that's all there is to it; then we won't be ashamed to
appear before the Lord each time he asks, 'Where
are you?'

When we speak of temptations, however, it is
easy to focus only on those that come to us from the
outside, but temptations also – and more often – come
from within us. We are inhabited by inner voices,
which make all sorts of suggestions to us, claiming
these are in our interest and will make us happy. But
if we actually listen to them, we find ourselves bound
hand and foot, and tightly bound, for these voices do
not come from the world of light, and the evil entities
that have won the day laugh at the poor innocent they
have managed to ensnare.

There is a Bulgarian fairytale which illustrates
this truth well. A man who was guilty of all sorts of
crimes – seducing and kidnapping women, robberies,
murders and so forth – was eventually caught and
sentenced to be hanged. As the rope was placed
around his neck, the devil appeared to him and asked,
'Can you see something over there?' – 'No.' – 'Look
harder.' – 'I can make out twenty mules.' – 'What
are they carrying on their backs?' – 'I'd say sandals,

a load of sandals.' – 'That's right,' said the devil, 'they are all the sandals I have worn out leading you to these gallows, where you're about to be hanged.' Those who are unable to resist all the voices speaking inside them that try to lead them astray will go to the gallows. There, the devil will show them all the sandals he has worn out getting them there. And there will be no point in blaming the devil, because human beings are always responsible for their own actions.

It's obvious that what we eat or drink always has consequences for us. When we're given a stimulant we become fidgety, when we're given a sedative we stay calm, and when we take a sleeping pill we go to sleep. In the same way, the mouldy bread, rotten fruit and bad wine tramps have to make do with not only destroy their body but also affect their moral life. Eating an exquisite dish or eating what gets thrown away will not have quite the same effect on our physical and psychological health.

But the state we are in when we eat is even more important, since we can also be poisoned by the healthiest and most succulent food if we fail to take certain precautions. How does this happen? If, as you bring the food to your mouth, you are troubled by problems, anger or other negative states, the food absorbs the poisons carried by these states and disperses them throughout your entire organism. Yes, you must be aware that, as you take your food in, it progressively absorbs the harmful elements you are sending out, and it poisons you. Of course, the opposite is true as well.[5]

It is normal to be momentarily troubled or irritated by certain events. But when this happens, even if it is your mealtime, wait a while before you eat until your inner peace and harmony have been restored. And if you cannot do this, if you have to eat right away, at least make the effort to concentrate on your food and imbue it with your respect and gratitude. These sentiments carried by the food as it enters you will transform your negative states.

So you see, here again Jesus' words are borne out: it is what comes out of our mouth, out of our astral mouth – our thoughts and feelings – that defiles us, because this also defiles what enters us – our food. But nothing that comes from outside can sully us if we are truly pure. A diamond, even when covered in mud, retains its purity and beauty; all you need do is wipe it for it to shine again in all its brilliance. And people who are truly spiritual can be compared to diamonds. Nothing can sully them unless they themselves renounce their diamond quality and allow themselves to revert to coal.

Sometimes, someone who has been reproached or criticized will say, 'It was a lot to swallow!' Isn't that so? It's an expression everyone knows and uses. Everyone knows, then, that there is a psychic mouth, an astral mouth. Through faith, love, wisdom, patience and all the other virtues, we can turn the raw, coarse, impure matter we receive into digestible food, and well enough to merit a diploma as a good cook. Some might say, 'What's so wonderful about a diploma in cooking?' Well, let's say a diploma in alchemy, if you prefer. There are many similarities between cooking and alchemy.[6]

As I have told you, nutrition is an inexhaustible subject, since it concerns the whole of our being. Everything we take in teaches us its secrets. To know is to introduce things and beings into oneself to study them. Nutrition is the key to knowledge: you must always begin by taking in what you want to know. The mouth is therefore the beginning, the first organ of wisdom.[7] It answers our questions about the nature of the foods we come across: do they have flavour, and what is that flavour? Are they beneficial for our health? The mouth, therefore, teaches us discernment.

By requiring all creatures, even the lowliest, to feed themselves, cosmic Intelligence obliges them to acquire at least some basic knowledge: through eating they begin to study the nature of things. In order to develop and learn, it is always necessary to begin by tasting. And what is true for microbes is even truer for human beings. But for us, of course, eating is not limited to the physical plane. The heart, mind, soul and spirit also need food. When you pray, meditate, read or study, when you contemplate the colours and beauty of nature or listen to music, what are you doing if not nourishing yourself on the higher planes? There, too, if you do not eat you become weak and die. Those who have no wish to study, pray or meditate are doomed to spiritual anaemia and die a spiritual death. This is the argument you can use with those who are lazy and have no wish to escape their psychic inertia: 'You don't want to eat? Well then, you'll die.'

But let's return to the two essential functions of the mouth: nutrition and speech. Food enters our mouth, and words come out of it. But is there no relationship between food and speech? Yes, there is, and this relationship is particularly clear in the figure of the Christ. The Christ is the Son, the second person of the Trinity, the creative Word uttered by the Father, and he also manifests as food, when Jesus says, *'I am the living bread that came down from heaven. Whoever eats of this bread will live for ever.'* Or again at the Last Supper, when Jesus gives the bread and wine to his disciples and says, *'Take, eat; this is my body... Drink, this is my blood.'*[8]

You will even find a passage in the Gospels where bread is clearly identified with the spoken word. When Jesus was hungry after fasting for forty days in the desert, the devil came to tempt him by suggesting he change stones into bread. But Jesus resisted him, saying, *'Man shall not live by bread alone, but by every word that proceeds from the mouth of God.'*[9]

On the spiritual plane, Christ is the Word of God. He is linked to God, just as words are linked to the person who utters them. And on the physical plane he is bread. This is another aspect of the relationship between the world below and the world above, between the physical world and the world of the spirit.

Notes

1. See *The Yoga of Nutrition,* Izvor 204, chap. 5: 'Vegetarianism'.
2. See *Les Deux Arbres du Paradis,* OC 3, chap. III: 'Ce que révèle le visage humain'.
3. See *The Fruits of the Tree of Life,* CW 32, chap. 11: 'The living logos'.
4. See *The Tree of the Knowledge of Good and Evil,* Izvor 210, chap. 1: 'The two trees of paradise'.
5. See *The Path of Silence,* Izvor 229, chap. 4: 'Make your meals an exercise in silence'.
6. See *True Alchemy or the Quest for Perfection,* Izvor 221.
7. See *The Second Birth,* CW 1, chap. 5: 'Love is hidden in the mouth'.
8. See *'Cherchez le Royaume de Dieu et sa Justice',* part VI, chap. 2-III: 'Celui qui mange ma chair et qui boit mon sang'.
9. See *'You are Gods',* Part II-3: 'The three great temptations'.

Chapter Three

'YOU ARE THE SALT OF THE EARTH'

I

Marking Matter with the Seal of the Spirit

Our physical body is made of matter, and because matter is subject to time it wears out and disintegrates. This is what we call ageing, and wrinkles, white hair, rheumatism and so on are all obvious signs of this process, which of course we don't like seeing. But we are not only a physical body, and though our body's ageing is in the natural order of things, nothing says we must age inwardly along with it. So there is really nothing to worry about!

In general, people who become really distressed by the signs of ageing they notice daily in the mirror are already old inside. Instead of worrying about maintaining what is warm and alive in themselves – their heart, in other words – they identify with their body, with matter. But it is their heart, not their body, that makes them young or old, and if their heart grows old it is because they allow it to happen. How? By losing their love for people and things, by losing their interest in and curiosity about the rich and abundant life that's there all around them.

Once they reach a certain age, many men and women believe they are old, speak of themselves as being old and let themselves go; they stop learning, stop inquiring and no longer make any effort. It's true that we meet elderly people who at eighty and ninety continue to be interested in everything and even take up studying. In my youth in Bulgaria I knew elderly people who were learning to read. They belonged to very poor families and had been unable to go to school. They married young, had children and worked hard all their life. Now in their old age their circumstances had improved, and because they now had more time to spare they were beginning to learn.

It is so touching to see an old grandfather or grandmother reciting the alphabet and spelling a very simple word! But very few follow this example. So many throw themselves on the scrap-heap to grow old and die. You will say you have known how to read and write for a long time. Of course you have, but there's always something new to learn, there are always efforts to be made, and it is only by doing this that you will stay young and alive.

In this day and age, in spite of enormous medical advances, illnesses which were once unknown are appearing in industrialized and prosperous countries. Why is this? And why do so many people suffer from depression, anxiety and nervous problems? It is because, even if they work for a living, humans always have a life of comfort, ease and pleasure as their ideal. But in fact, nowhere in nature is there a blueprint for an easy life. Comfort, ease and the pursuit of pleasure introduce the germs of illness into humans and annihilate life itself. Their cells become lazy; they no longer eliminate impurities and become polluted, and the organism loses its ability to resist illness. Be wary of ease, comfort and pleasure; drive this ideal from your mind, for in reality it brings death.

Human beings are on earth to work, and when I say 'work' I mean first and foremost to work on themselves, to strive to go beyond themselves, to surpass themselves. Of course, we see people go to work every day, but the purpose of all their efforts is mostly to ensure their survival, their well-being, their material security; for this reason, yes, they are willing to work. But they are not so ready to work on their thinking so they can become masters of all circumstances. They count on an easy life, in which nothing difficult or painful will happen to them. The Lord himself will protect them, providing them with tranquillity and good health; this is even what they pray to him for. As for non-believers, it's society that they expect to help and protect them. So they take out insurance against accidents, theft, fire, flood and so on, and if an unforeseen problem or misfortune befalls them, they go before the courts to be recognized as victims and demand compensation: they should have been spared!

No, it's about time humans knew that, whatever they think or do, they will never be totally sheltered and protected. If this is what they want, they shouldn't come to earth, because life on earth is a risky business for everyone without exception. We are on earth to learn, to progress, and the difficulties and tests are there precisely to force us to do so; we cannot escape them. So instead of rushing around making demands, protesting and complaining, each of us must carry out inner work, for it is within ourselves first of all that we will find remedies, compensation, consolation and hope.

A minimum of comfort and material convenience is obviously essential. But if you wish to preserve the true life in yourself, do not give too much importance to comfort, whether material or moral, or laziness will be lying in wait for you, and laziness links you to currents which numb you and hinder your evolution. Try to put down all your cumbersome baggage, all your concerns about material things which are not absolutely necessary, so you are always able to go further and higher.[1]

It is work that fortifies us; it is work that reinforces us, as long as it's accompanied by an idea. Every gesture you infuse with a divine idea is inscribed in the archives of your higher consciousness, from which all positive energies then spring forth: joy, purity, light and peace. Yes, however modest, every task you undertake with the conviction that you are participating in the proper order of things, in the harmony of earth and the harmony of heaven, strengthens you.

Even in daily life, what weakens and destroys human beings is their ignorance of the right state of mind to adopt when carrying out certain tasks. Either they don't like what they have to do and complain about it, or they think it should be the responsibility of others and they are being taken advantage of, etc. In these conditions, of course, the slightest obligation becomes an intolerable burden. But if you set to work with the conviction that you are doing something good for yourself and for others, that you are contributing to the successful functioning of the whole to which you belong, notice what happens: you are able to continue a long time without tiring.

Of course, you must be sensible and not throw yourself headlong into back-breaking tasks. What I am referring to here are your daily activities. Make every effort to carry these out in the best possible frame of mind. Otherwise, you would do better to stop, because a state of dissatisfaction produces a poison that saps the body's energy.

I am not against material progress that makes life easier and more comfortable, but comfort as most people live it is dangerous, because it goes against the activity of the spirit. Because all physical activity is related to the spirit, this form of passivity, of laziness even, which is favoured by technical progress, hampers the faculties of the spirit.

Whether you like the idea or not, discomfort stimulates intelligence, the need for creativity. Most of the great masterpieces of humanity have been created in discomfort. And are we no longer creating masterpieces today, you may ask? Yes, but the masterpieces of our times are no longer masterpieces of art or thought but of extremely sophisticated appliances and machines. Appliances and machines are the most remarkable achievements of our era, and it is true that they command our admiration, but, however admirable, they are in the process of paralysing and chloroforming human beings.

We are on earth to develop ourselves, and developing ourselves means exercising the power of the spirit over matter: not just the matter outside ourselves but, especially, the matter within us. And we will know how to master external matter only when we have first learned to master our inner matter; otherwise we will be crushed. This is the meaning of Jesus' words to his disciples in the Sermon on the Mount: *'You are the salt of the earth; but if the salt loses its flavour, how shall it be seasoned? It is then good for nothing but to be thrown out and trampled underfoot.'* And the possible applications of this saying are vast!

'You are the salt of the earth.' How are we to understand the word 'salt'?

Salt comes from the sea and is therefore connected to the mystery of our origins. Even the most ignorant of human beings know just how precious salt is. Our body absolutely needs salt, and many foods would seem insipid and bland if we didn't add a little to them. In Bulgaria, as in other countries, I expect, it is traditional to offer bread and salt as a sign of welcome.

Not only does salt give taste to our foods, it also has the property of preserving them; in other words, it prevents them from going bad. So it is linked to the idea of purification and is used in certain religious ceremonies – in Christian baptism, for example, where the priest puts a few grains of salt on the infant's lips. As far back as the Old Testament, there is a passage in which the prophet Elijah purifies the water of a spring by throwing salt into it. But, for the Hebrews, salt was above all a symbol of their covenant with God. When God instructed Moses on the ritual of sacrifice, he told him, *'You shall not omit from your grain-offerings the salt of the covenant with your God; with all your offerings you shall offer salt.'*

As salt is linked to purification, it is also used in the rites of exorcism to chase away demons and free people from spells and black magic. In Bulgaria I again heard this recommendation: 'Against black magic, salt and water!' So, essentially, there is no difference between certain religious rites and rites of magic. The purpose of the ceremony of baptism, in which the priest pours water over the infant and places salt on its lips, is to wash away the infant's original sin and protect its soul from attacks by the devil.[2] Most rites in the Christian religion, like those in other religions, are rites of magic. This is why I am always astonished to see the look of horror on Christians' faces when they hear me use the word 'magic'. But of course magic is a domain you must enter with great caution, and above all you must see that you use its methods only for good, so that you manifest as a white magician and bring peace and light wherever you go.[3]

But let's come back to the words of Jesus. Given salt's powers and virtues, when Jesus said to his disciples, *'You are the salt of the earth'*, it meant he was entrusting them with a very great mission. And he entrusts this same mission to us as well. It's as if he were saying to us, 'Thanks to you, the earth will take on flavour. You will preserve everything that is good and beautiful, and you will give meaning to life. For this is what flavour means. You are bearers of the meaning of life, which I represent, and because of you everything in the world will take on meaning. Remain vigilant, therefore, and do not put yourself in situations where you will lose this quality that salt possesses, for you will no longer have mastery over events, and you will be crushed.'

Philosophers write endless essays on the meaning of life, when really it is very simple: the meaning of life lies in the flavour we find in things, and it is the spirit, yes, the spirit within us, which gives them this flavour.[4]

It is said of some people that they have a zest, a charm, something indefinable that attracts our attention and makes us seek them out. We feel drawn by their 'salt', which adds flavour to their words, their looks and their gestures. However, as they are not always aware that this is a gift from heaven that they must preserve, they give themselves over to a prosaic existence and lose their salt. They become petty and dull, and others no longer want to seek them out. Then they suffer and complain, 'No one loves me anymore; no one even knows I exist.' Yes, they have lost their salt.

We can think of salt as a condensation of the earth's magnetism: it is from this that salt's virtues and power of attraction are derived. We too have been given these virtues and power of attraction by God, and we must not only preserve them but also find out how to develop them. Yes, you should understand that salt represents all the powers the Creator has placed in our spirit, all the elements he has given us to enable us to provide for our needs without always having to go looking for something outside ourselves.

Now that science and technology have given them the possibility to do so, our contemporaries are throwing themselves headlong into exploiting all the resources the physical world offers them. And yet, if they agreed to further develop their inner potential, not only would they have less need to plunder the planet's resources and exploit their fellow humans but they would realize that their inner wealth, unlike their material wealth, is inexhaustible, infinite.

On all sides, you hear loud complaints about how people are becoming increasingly materialistic. And what is extraordinary is that even materialists complain about it! Why? Because for those who complain, it is always others who are the materialists. Their own aspirations are high and altruistic, whereas

others are egotistical, greedy and unscrupulous!
Yes, it is extraordinary how few people realize
that they themselves possess the same materialistic
tendencies they point out in others. And many who
call themselves spiritual should analyse themselves
a little more carefully.

The fact that we endlessly experience new needs
is, of course, a sign of evolution. Not to want anything,
not to have a taste for anything, to live without trying
to gain something more each day isn't particularly
good. But the greed and voraciousness with which so
many people seek satisfaction on the physical level
will only drag humanity into catastrophe. And why
is it that even those who are aware of this persist
on the same path? It's quite simple: because they
don't know themselves. If they knew the Creator had
placed within them, at a subtle level, the equivalent
of everything that can be found in the universe,
instead of plundering the earth they would nourish
themselves and beautify themselves with the riches
they found within, the riches of the spirit. And then
everything they achieved on the physical level would
be marked with the seal of the spirit. Perhaps this
idea is difficult for many to understand, but I'll give
you a very simple example that will doubtless remind
some of you of your own experiences.

When you consult a doctor, you may find
that they are quite satisfied merely to prescribe
medication. In the practice of their profession, they
make use of knowledge acquired from books. They
examine their patients exactly the way a mechanic

examines a car that's broken down, and their care will certainly produce results. But now take a doctor who is truly motivated by the need to help others, to soothe their ills and comfort them: their goodness and compassion are so strong, they permeate their whole way of being. So when they are with their patients, what emanates from their look, their voice and their handshake awakens powers in the patient's heart and soul which will act imperceptibly on their physical body. So, it's these subtle elements emanating from the doctor that have a healing effect on the sick, awakening in them certain energies that will act beneficially on their organism.

But that is just one example; the clergy with the faithful, parents and educators with children, bosses with employees: in all walks of life we notice that what emanates from the very depth of a person's being influences the psychic matter, and consequently the behaviour, of those they relate to. You must have noticed this yourself. Aren't there people you love to see and meet, because you have the impression that as a result of your contact with them you become a better person, more intelligent, more trusting of life, and that you feel better physically as well?

Well, since you have established that elements from the subtle planes can stimulate such beneficial states of awareness in you, decide now to begin searching deep within yourself for what you need, instead of always looking for it externally in the physical world. Not only will you be less likely to grab what belongs to others or what they need more than you do, also, because the source of the riches inside you is inexhaustible, it will take only a very few things to make you happy, satisfied and fulfilled, to quench your thirst. You see, we always come back to the same question: how can we free the spirit within us, this spirit Jesus calls *'the salt of the earth'*?

We must count on ourselves, on the spirit within us. Yes, the spirit, because in times of trial and turmoil, when we feel abandoned and rejected, only the spirit has the power to calm us, console us and give us the means to rebuild ourselves. We can be completely abandoned, we can lose everything, everything except ourselves, our spirit. Then why not look within ourselves, since this is the only real possession, the only real certainty we have? Whether we are on the earth or in the other world, we will always be with ourselves, inseparable.

So that we may remain masters of the situation in every circumstance, we all have something at our disposal that nothing and no one can take from us. And this something that nothing and no one can take from us is ourselves. In life and in death, we will be with ourselves for eternity. Yes, it's the one thing we can be absolutely certain of; all the rest is uncertain and can slip through our fingers. And this 'self' that nothing can take away is our consciousness of the divine spark that we are, our consciousness, therefore, of the capacities we have received from the Creator and the opportunities we are given each day to put them to work.

Everything that happens to us takes on meaning and value only in so far as we are resolved to put it to good use. When we do so, even failure and disgrace are transformed into precious stones. Success and honours, on the other hand, eventually turn against us if we fail to nurture a great ideal in our heart that will enable us to use them for the good.[5]

Heaven makes use of everything to urge humans to seek this salt that will revitalize and purify the earth: their own earth to begin with, and then all the earths around them. But as they gradually settle into their lives, so many men and women allow their salt to lose its flavour! As soon as they count for something in society, they think only of consolidating their position and their gains. Considering themselves to be the sole author of their success, they cut their link with the divine Source. Very few are aware of all the blessings each day can bring when they strive to live in the light of the spirit. They realize this only when they have lost this light, just as they only truly appreciate their health when they have lost it.

The Creator has placed in humans everything they need to face every situation in life. You must work with this truth your entire life. Whatever happens, whatever your difficulties and tests, remember that God has equipped you with a kind of laboratory where you can go and work. Here in your inner laboratory you will find liquids, powders and gasses, as well as directions for using them. Even the destitute, even reprobates and criminals possess all the elements necessary to regenerate themselves. Because they have accumulated mountains of obstacles in themselves, it's now very difficult for them to overcome these and gain access to their laboratory, but it is there inside them, and one day they will gain entry to it.

For two thousand years Christians have continued to say that God is love, but what have they really understood of this truth? To say that God is love is to be aware that he has given everything to all beings, without exception. You suffer and are unhappy, and you pray to God to come to your aid. You think you need his help right now and he should give it to you. Well, you are wrong. There's nothing God should be doing for you now, because he has already done everything. When he created human beings, he anticipated everything and gave them everything. So do not ask for anything else. True sons and daughters of God are those who ask for nothing, knowing they already have everything. It is ridiculous to ask for hands to work with, feet to walk with and eyes to see with, since you already have them on the spiritual plane, just as you do on the physical plane. You must only pray to ask how best to use them, and the light will tell you.[6]

Whatever our apparent insufficiencies at the moment, in reality we lack nothing. And with what we have we can draw closer to saintliness each day, to that state of purity and light which is the attribute of God himself,[7] as the Seraphim who stand before his throne endlessly repeat: *'Holy, holy, holy, is the Lord God...'* But God has provided for us so completely that he has also given us elements that go against saintliness. We must work to transform these elements, for this is how we will reach true saintliness. Saintliness is a state we attain in full consciousness. What advantage would we gain from walking the path of good like robots, without knowing why or how we were doing it? In order to appreciate the light, it is necessary to have conquered the darkness, for our knowledge of the light will be enriched by our knowledge of the darkness.

The day you become conscious of the truth that everything you need you already have in your possession, you will discover how rich you are. Why don't you drill for oil? It will gush forth. Why don't you mine your earth? You'll discover precious stones in it. But you wait and do nothing. You are like beggars who pester passers-by: you endlessly importune the Lord and his angels.

With the technical means now at their disposal, chemists are able to extract lots of substances from metals and minerals (and the same with plants) for use in the manufacture of different products. But it doesn't end there: more and more they will penetrate the secret treasures of nature, discovering that everything that exists is composed of elements endowed with particular beneficial properties. You have only to look at pharmaceutical products: they all come from one kingdom of nature or another. To distinguish them from natural products, some are called chemical products, but whatever the chemical product it has its origins in nature.

And the human being is equally part of nature. So, resolve to delve into the immense laboratory that you are, where all the elements you need for your physical, psychic and spiritual development are assembled. There's nothing to prevent you from looking for these elements outside yourself, but never forget that everything is within you, and that you must strive to acquire and develop the awareness of your riches and powers. The day you truly experience yourself as being the bearer of all these elements, you will begin to focus on this inner treasure.

Today I would like you to steep yourself in this truth, which is the most important truth for your evolution. It has already been expressed, though inadequately, here and there in books by various authors, and it is this truth that Jesus makes us look at when he says, *'You are the salt of the earth.'* So go deep in yourself to find all the riches God has placed there. Of course, these riches are not very apparent. The most precious of what God has given us is deeply hidden and invisible. Why? Because God is a very wise father; if he had laid out all these riches before humans, they would make no effort and would be content merely to take. And how would they use these riches, since they wouldn't know their value? But when they are forced to take the trouble to discover them, they know how to appreciate them and use them for the good.

Whatever your circumstances, acquire the habit of going within yourself to find the quintessences we know as love, wisdom, gentleness, goodness, peace, inspiration, purity and gratitude. Simple objects you take in your hand can help bring what is hidden in the deepest part of you to the surface – a bird's feather, the leaf of a tree, a pebble... everything can become an intermediary, a means of entering into relationship with your inner world. A written word will also do: you write the word on a sheet of paper, and as a result of repeating this one word, you enter your inner laboratory where you find the flask bearing the same name. This written word is like a witness, a detector; you hold it in one hand, and with the other you look for the flask, and because there is an affinity between this word and a particular flask you eventually find it. I'll never stop telling you this: there are so many things at your disposal, if only you made the effort to use them!

Notes

1. See *'Et il me montra un fleuve d'eau de la vie'*, Part XII: 'Et sur les deux bords du fleuve il y avait un arbre de vie'.
2. See *'Cherchez le Royaume de Dieu et sa Justice'*, Part VI, chap. 2, II: 'Les pouvoirs de l'eau'.
3. See T*he Book of Divine Magic*, Izvor 226.
4. See *The Seeds of Happiness*, Izvor 231, chap. 6: 'The meaning of life'.
5. See *Youth: Creators of the Future*, Izvor 233, chap. 8: 'Learning to handle success and failure'.
6. See *The Faith That Moves Mountains*, Izvor 238, chap. 3: 'Faith and belief'.
7. See *'Cherchez le Royaume de Dieu et sa Justice'*, Part 1, pp. 18-19.

II

The Source of Energy

One day the Master Peter Deunov said, 'You are complaining of an empty stomach, because you have had to make do with quarter of a loaf of bread. It is not really your stomach that is empty but your head and your heart. The bread contains enough salt to nourish you for a long time if you accompany every mouthful with a wise thought and a loving feeling. So do not disregard this small amount of salt, for great treasures are contained within it.'

How should we interpret these words of the Master? Is he really saying we should make do with quarter of a loaf of bread each day? Of course not! He simply wants us to understand that the most important way to nourish ourselves well is with quality, not quantity. But true quality is difficult to find, because we won't find it provided in any shop. Quality is an element which must come from ourselves.

It is important to eat enough food and to eat healthy food, but it is up to each of us to add an element from ourselves to the simplest food in order to give it flavour – flavour that will be a source of energy. A simple piece of bread can thus become an exquisite, life-giving food. There are ways to add qualities to what we eat, and I want to turn my attention to this seemingly insignificant point.[1] But let's begin by studying what the Master Peter Deunov calls 'salt', since this will help us go deeper still into Jesus' words: *'You are the salt of the earth.'*

Beyond the earth's atmosphere, in what the ancients called the ether, there is a vital substance distributed throughout space. And everything that exists on earth, beings as well as things, has the ability to attract and retain a certain amount of this life-bearing substance. It is contained in food, air, heat and light, and we absorb it in different ways. It is to be hoped that even scientists will look into this matter and that their laboratory research will enlighten us as to the nature of this quintessence, this 'salt' which is so vital for our physical, psychic and spiritual health. The Hindus call this salt *prana* and have methods for capturing it, especially through respiration.[2]

But there are many methods besides respiration, such as the contemplation of the sunrise and of the starry sky at night. Contact with the forces of nature in the forests, mountains, rivers, lakes and seas provides another method, as does nutrition, for all the foods we eat contain something of this quintessence, which is distributed throughout space, from the rocks to the stars.

So let us turn our attention once more to nutrition, which affords us daily possibilities for collecting this 'salt' with which the sun impregnates all earth's produce by means of its rays. Vegetables and fruits are all full of it, but are you aware of this? No, you are interested in them only because you need them to keep you going. Naturally, you choose those that are pleasant to the taste, but you are unaware of what they represent. During meals your preoccupations mostly bear no relation to the act of eating. From now on, try to have some regard for what you have put on your plate, and at least say, 'Thank you, Lord, for allowing me to taste you through these vegetables and fruits, which carry your life.' And these vegetables and fruits will rejoice at being appreciated as bearers of the divine life.

Of course, you don't take this very seriously, and instead of my lingering yet again on the subject of nutrition, no doubt you would prefer me to tell you how to become rich or successful in your profession, or how to attract love. Well, if you really knew how to listen to me, you would understand that wealth and success are all I do speak about. I explain a very deep truth to you in the simplest way: if you become conscious of food as a bearer of the divine life, you will introduce thoughts and feelings into your head and heart capable of attracting and collecting the salt that gives true flavour. And when you possess this salt, what else could you wish for?

Thought and feeling act on the functioning of glands throughout our body, especially the salivary glands. Once activated, these glands secrete chemical elements which extract energy from the food. It is not the stomach but the mouth and tongue that receive the quintessence of foods, thanks to our feelings of love and the thoughts that accompany them. The tongue and mouth are equipped to draw what is essential and vital from our food and send it to the brain as well as to the entire nervous system. So even before the food passes into the stomach and then on into the intestines, the body has already absorbed their etheric elements, those that provide vitality.

The proof is that when you haven't eaten for twenty-four or forty-eight hours and then are given a piece of fruit, no sooner do you taste it than your thoughts become more lucid and your feelings warmer, and you feel joy and hope. Where has this energy come from? Before the food reaches the stomach to be digested, the nervous system has already been nourished.

But have any scientists taken the time to study this subtle aspect of nutrition?[3] When physicists reveal they can extract enough energy from the atom – this infinitesimal particle of matter – to run powerful machines, the whole world marvels. But who takes any notice of the fact that a similar phenomenon occurs in nutrition, of which we are, every day, both the agents and the beneficiaries? No one is interested or even believes that taking in a small particle of matter is enough to fill our entire being with pure energy. But tell me why a human being, who has been created in the image of God, should be less capable than experts in nuclear physics?

Now you understand why the Master Peter Deunov said, 'It is not your stomach which is empty but your head and your heart.' For it is through your thoughts and feelings that you draw this salt from your food, the salt which gives you real force, real energy. This is a law of the spiritual life: in order to fully benefit from what you receive, you must add to it something of your soul and your spirit.

But while you are looking to fill your reservoirs with this salt of life, watch that you do not lose from one hand what you have just gained with the other. Anger, for example, causes a great loss of force, exhausting the nervous system. When you feel anger or exasperation rising in you, how many of you think of channelling this energy, of using it to light up your town or turn your millwheel? (You obviously have to transpose these images…) Most people let themselves get carried away and then boast, 'Hey! I taught that idiot a real lesson!' With their angry outburst, they said what they thought, of course, but, more than that, they drained themselves and will need a great deal of time to recoup this wasted energy.[4]

But anger is only one example. There are many other situations where you waste precious energy! Take malicious gossip, for example, which is such a widespread failing. To talk and complain about others, to criticize them, accuse them and meddle in their affairs exhausts the brain and the heart.

So it is up to you to examine yourself and notice in which situations your strength goes or returns and to analyse what causes this. Also find out which foods and drinks stimulate you, reinforce you and make you feel light and, on the other hand, which make you feel heavy and lethargic. Some animals can be captured easily after a meal, because digestion makes them drowsy, and in the same way after certain meals humans can also succumb to drowsiness, which exposes them as prey. These are meals they take on the lower astral and lower mental planes, offered to them by the dark entities of the invisible world. And what meals they are! There is a whole parade of dishes and wines which they find particularly delicious. And what are these dishes and wines? Ambition, sensuality, jealousy, vengeance, betrayal, hatred…

Every day evil entities try to tempt humans with this sort of feast, luring them into their traps so they can seize them and drain them of their divine energy. So be vigilant, observe yourself, and gradually the reality of this energy given you by God will become obvious to you, and you will make every effort to protect it and increase it.

You all have very practical meters in your houses; as they turn, they record the precise amount of gas, water and electricity you have consumed. An employee comes regularly to read the numbers on the meter, and you can't dodge the issue: the quantities are recorded, and you have to pay the sum corresponding to what you have consumed. Well, long before they existed in our houses, these meters existed in humans themselves. Yes, you possess the three meters for water, gas and electricity; not only this but there are also employees who come to take readings. Cosmic Intelligence has thought of everything.

The water meter is the mouth; on your lips is recorded the amount of water you have caused to flow. Water corresponds to feelings, and the employee who knows how to read the signs can tell from your mouth whether you have been economical or wasteful but also whether you have respected or transgressed any laws. For this meter, which registers quantity, also reveals quality: it tells whether or not the water is clean and rich in life-giving elements. Everything is precisely noted.

The gas meter is the nose. The nose allows us to understand the importance human beings give to thought and to assess the use they make of it. For it is not enough to think. You must consider the rightness of your thoughts and assess their consequences for yourself and others: do they light the way? Are they constructive and creative?

The electricity meter corresponds to the eyes, which show whether the currents running through the nervous system have been harmonious or chaotic. And if the mouth is linked to the element of water and the nose to the element of air, the eyes are linked to fire and thus to light. It is the eyes that receive light – physical light – but we can also read in people's gaze whether they know how to receive and give spiritual light.

It is essential to learn how to conserve and even enhance one's energy while remaining as active as possible.[5] For work is also a source of energy, and you can prolong your life if you know how to work. Many people work in an agitated, feverish, tense state, which only exhausts them. Whether from a need to hurry, or because someone has instilled in them the belief that work is the greatest virtue, they never stop rushing about, and they end up upsetting their stomach, their liver, their nervous system... Even the objects they handle suffer from this feverishness. It is not enough to know that work prolongs life. You must learn to work in balance and harmony, so you can draw from each activity a few grains of this salt that gives life its real flavour.

Notes
1. See *The Yoga of Nutrition,* Izvor 204, chap. 9: 'The meaning of the blessing' and chap. 10: 'The Spirit transforms matter'.
2. See *'Cherchez le Royaume de Dieu et sa Justice',* part III, chap. 5: 'Respirer: s'accorder aux rythmes de l'univers'.
3. See *Hrani yoga, le sens alchimique et magique de la nutrition,* OC 16.
4. See *'You are Gods',* part VII, chap. 2: 'The solar plexus'.
5. See *Harmony and Health,* Izvor 225, chap. 8: 'How to become tireless'.

Chapter Four

'BUT IF THE SALT LOSES ITS FLAVOUR…'

What are we doing on earth? What is our reason for coming here? We have come with a very important purpose: to study matter and to work with the forces that animate it. We are spirits who have been given a body so that we can operate in matter. Some people think the Lord arranged things very badly: since man and woman are spirits, it would have been better for them to have remained in the world of spirit, in the light and magnificence of heaven, instead of incarnating in bodies which limit and imprison them. No, the Lord in his great wisdom decided otherwise, and despite appearances our descent into matter does not exile us far from him, for matter belongs to the very essence of God; it is a condensation of the divine force.

Try to follow closely now while I explain. When we study the different kingdoms of nature, we see that each one serves as food for the kingdom directly above it. So, minerals serve as food for plants: through their roots, plants absorb and elaborate elements contained in the soil. Plants are therefore the first workers responsible for transforming matter. They give it movement, for they themselves possess movement. They are able to grow and to turn towards the light, and their flowers open and close... But plants in their turn serve as food for animals: through them, vegetable matter receives greater vitality and sensitivity.

Humans, in turn, eat animals, and in doing so they also cause them to evolve. You may say, 'But if we help animals to evolve by eating them, why do you advocate vegetarianism?' Wait, don't rush to put steak or poultry on your menu under the pretext of helping cows, chickens and turkeys to evolve. Feeding on animals does not necessarily mean eating their flesh. We can simply use their produce: their milk, from which we make butter and cheese, their eggs, their honey, and so forth.

But let's get back to the point. Matter, which is inert in stones, receives movement by way of plants, then sensitivity by way of animals, and finally thought by way of human beings. But the process does not stop there, since humans also serve as food for other entities: the angels. And how do the angels feed on us? In their own way, they too are 'vegetarians': they take our good thoughts, our good feelings, everything in us inspired by wisdom and love, by the spirit of abnegation and sacrifice.

Angels see us as plants which produce flowers and fruits. When they come to pick our flowers and fruits, they do not break our branches. On the contrary, they water us, care for us and bring us all their blessings so that the fruits we give will be even more succulent. Of course, there are also 'angels' of another kind: dark entities and demons. Like all living creatures, they too must eat, and they feast on those humans whose evil schemes and feelings of hatred, jealousy and rebellion make tasty dishes for them; they rob them of all their energy, leaving them drained. Nothing is more desirable than to serve as food for the angels of light, and nothing is worse than being devoured by the spirits of darkness.[1]

And since angels are also made of matter, a very subtle matter, they in turn serve as food for the archangels, and the archangels for the principalities, and so on, by way of the virtues, the powers, the dominions, the thrones and the cherubim. This matter becomes more and more subtle, until it reaches the seraphim, who prepare it to serve as food for God himself.[2]

So, from stone to God, what we see is the evolution of matter. This evolution passes by way of humans and is the profound reason for their incarnation in a physical body. Otherwise, it is true, they might just as well have remained on high in light and bliss. For this reason, all beings who do not seek to perfect themselves by working on their own matter regress until they return to the mineral stage, to stone. Do you understand this?

God's love is infinite. Like beams radiating from his heart, this love waters, sustains and revitalizes all creatures, leading them to perfection. But if they do not allow themselves to be penetrated by the spiritual forces which work in matter to animate it, to make it more sensitive and more receptive to the light from above, they die, for that is what death really is. We must understand death as a refusal to evolve, a refusal to vibrate in unison with the currents of the spirit.[3]

Death is a fall into the densest, most compact matter, and this fall takes place in people's consciousness: they lose the light, they lose the memory of the heavenly imprint inscribed within them, and they become stones, in which life has slowed down to such a degree that it no longer has the force to produce thoughts and feelings. Life is a perpetual movement forward, and those who refuse to go forward regress, returning to the unconsciousness of the stone, which is simply consciousness asleep. All of their physical and psychic manifestations express this petrified life.[4]

Deep within stone, however, something of the divine spark still exists. In the stones and soil we walk on, beings exist that were once endowed with movement, feeling and thought but descended so far into matter that we now trample them underfoot. This is how the words of Jesus can be explained: *'If the salt loses its flavour… it is then good for nothing but to be thrown out and trampled underfoot.'* Those who have lost their ideal, their light, their salt, have been thrown out. Symbolically speaking, the outside is matter, and the inside is spirit. All creatures who have lost their salt and abandoned the spirit are trampled underfoot. All societies, nations and families which have lost their salt are trampled underfoot. For what purpose? To force them to find their flavour again.

Of course, the point of view I am expressing here will seem senseless to many, and no geologist or palaeontologist would accept it. And yet, it is the truth. We walk on beings that lost their salt sometime in the past. You may not choose to believe me, but that doesn't make it any less true. What do we know of the peoples that preceded us?

In order to move the inert matter of stones, God created plants, about which many things are still unknown to science. Plants are intelligent entities, but because their soul floats far above them in space, we are unable to communicate with them as we can with animals, or as we can to an even greater extent with humans, who are inhabited by an individual soul.[5]

Through plants the first ray of God's love is made manifest. Plants are the first to bring inert matter to life, and they speak to it like this: 'O you creatures who live in stones, you have been there for billions of years, and you think you have been abandoned. But God is thinking of you, and little by little you will again take up the path of light. It will take a long time, but you will succeed.' And they continue working on mineral matter to soften and moisten it. Then come animals, who continue the elaboration, followed by humans... In this way matter is vivified, enriched and illuminated.

It is the mission of humans to transform matter with the power of the spirit. But so many men and women still remain numb and immobilized! They consider it normal to be in this stone-like state; in fact, they are not even aware of it. And yet it is clear that what characterizes stones is their inability to move. You always have to push them, if you want them to change position. And one day they are broken up by great hammer blows and made into roads, bridges, houses and so on.

Each of you, therefore, must at least strive to leave the mineral kingdom to become a plant and grow, and later you can learn to move without having to be picked or pulled up. Look at all the advantages there are in being autonomous and moving about without outside intervention! Animals can look for food, escape danger and take shelter in bad weather. The day humans develop these possibilities in their inner life, they will have made great progress. But it will still remain for them to enter the human kingdom fully, in other words to enter the world of thought and reason, in order to become masters of their destiny.

'You are the salt of the earth, but if the salt loses its flavour… it is then good for nothing but to be thrown out and trampled underfoot…' Salt represents the quintessence of the earth, and if you lose your flavour you too will be thrown out. And what will happen then? You will become chemical fertilizer, and you will suffer. When human beings lose their flavour, nothing else has any flavour either.

No matter what they do, everything is dull, boring and sad. Even if they eat and drink the most delicious things, even if they have multiple marriages and sexual conquests, it's meaningless to them; they have no more taste for anything. Why have they lost their taste for people and things? Because they have given in to a life of ease, because all their efforts have become focused on material acquisitions and pleasures. They have abandoned the spirit in themselves and lost the meaning of life, the taste for life; they have become no more than stones. What can be done with such people? Even the Lord can do nothing for them.

You'll say, 'But if they meet an initiate, a great sage…' Initiates and sages are not all-powerful, as they themselves know, which is why they only take an interest in those who represent plants, animals or humans on the ladder of evolution. What can be done with stones, since they don't move? But presented with a plant, a sage will say, 'I will look after it, I will plant it in the ground, and it will develop. From time to time, of course, I will have to water it and feed it, but it will grow.' As for animals, they are able to provide food for themselves, which is even better.

A spiritual master cannot take an interest in humans who have remained stones. There is no point, for they always need to be pushed and given new impetus if they are to move.[6] Once this impetus wears off, they stop, until they receive a new boost from outside. Even if a plant also needs a little water and fertilizer, it will continue to grow when it receives a boost. But a stone... When you push it, it rolls a bit and stops dead. What a lot of energy expended for next to no result!

Some people will be surprised and even indignant: 'What? A spiritual master should have enough love to take an interest in everyone!' Unfortunately, great as his love may be, a master can do nothing for those who are stones and wish to remain stones. If he is to do anything, these stones must at least have the desire to become plants. If they are happy with their condition as stones, no one will persuade them to change.

Ask even the most patient and dedicated teachers whether they can get children to learn anything when they remain stubbornly closed to everything they are taught and use any excuse to miss school. We have to wait for life to give these children a few knocks to get them to understand all they have lost by not wanting to be instructed. Well, it's the same with certain people: life will shake them up, even break them into pieces, until they understand they are stones that must at least become plants.

These comparisons between human beings and the different kingdoms of nature are obviously oversimplified, but they are true. People who allow themselves to become absorbed in material concerns bind themselves to the mineral world, and even their facial features become fixed and coarse. Others who overflow with vitality become like plants, and nothing can stop them growing. Those who are governed by their instinctual impulses and their emotions are still at the animal stage, but if they study and reflect they will enter the kingdom of human beings! As for attaining the angelic kingdom, they will succeed in that only when they give priority to the spirit: to the light and force of the spirit.

Now, do not misunderstand me. Although human beings inwardly have to drag themselves away from the inertia of the mineral world, this does not mean that stones are unworthy of our respect. Stones are living beings. Since the entire universe is alive with God's life, stones are also alive, which means they can experience delight and even think. You may say that, unlike plants, they have not been given an etheric body, much less an astral or mental body, and therefore can neither feel delight nor think… It's true that stones have no etheric, astral or mental body, and if we place them at the bottom of the evolutionary ladder it is because their spiritual being is so far removed it has no communication with them. Stones are receptacles for a spiritual being, but this being has not descended far enough into them to animate them.

Plants have been given an etheric body by the spirit, and animals have been given both an etheric body and an astral body. As for humans, because the spirit has incarnated even more deeply in them, they have been given a mental body as well. The extent to which the spirit has descended into creatures to manifest itself is the criterion for the degree of evolution. It is very simple. In humans, or at least in some of them, the spirit has penetrated deeply. In stones, we can scarcely perceive the slightest movement.

But is there really such a contrast between a human being and a stone? No, in an absolute sense a stone is not inferior to a human being. And what is it in the stone that experiences delight and thinks? It is the spirit on high and not the stone itself.. When you move or break stones, they rejoice because they sense they are going to take part in the construction of something new. When we were in the mountains of Rila with the Master Peter Deunov, he sometimes asked us to water the stones. He explained to us that occasionally they needed our help, that they too were linked to other creatures in the world and could be visited by higher beings.

Because science studies only one aspect of nature – its anatomy – it draws erroneous conclusions from these studies. To be complete and true, it must also study the other two aspects – physiological and psychological – as the initiates and true poets do.

So there you have a few words about stones.

Stones are true to the mission the Creator has given them. But the Creator has given us humans another mission: to bring down the spirit so that it lives within us. To achieve this, we must devote more time to prayer and meditation, and we must increase our love, so that what is dead in us revives. We have great efforts to make and great difficulties to overcome before the spirit can deeply penetrate the matter of our inner being. But this is our work: to

awaken the powers the Creator has placed in us, so
we may fully realize our divine destiny.

Never have I expressed to you so simply what our
work consists of. You can no longer say you don't
know what you have to do. You just have to want to
do it. In fact, when you claim not to be clear what the
work consists of, what it really means is you don't
want to work. You are simply being dishonest with
yourself. Those who truly want to work receive the
necessary instruction and advice. Those who don't
will be like the salt that has lost its flavour, and they
will have to endure great suffering in order to find it
again. This is the meaning of the other passage in the
Gospels in which Jesus mentions salt: *'For everyone
will be salted with fire.'*

What is the relationship between salt and fire?
Fire, like salt, is a symbol of the spirit. And like
fire, salt burns, but fire exists in different forms and
therefore has different ways of burning. You may
remember that years ago I talked to you about three
kinds of fire. Reread this lecture.[7] Fire is synonymous
with life, but also with suffering and death. Fire
sustains life but also has the power to destroy it, and
to destroy it so totally that nothing remains. It is the
same with salt: it is strongly linked with the origins
of life, and it also has the power to destroy life. What
the ancient Hebrews called the Salt Sea we today call
the Dead Sea, for the salt has destroyed all vegetation
in it. In the Old Testament, when God wants to
punish humans for their wickedness, *'he turns… a*

fruitful land into a salty waste.' In the same way, he causes sulphur, salt and fire to fall upon Sodom and Gomorrah and turns Lot's wife into a pillar of salt for disobeying his orders.

Salt, like fire, can therefore serve both as the bearer of death and the bearer of life. Thus, when Jesus says, *'Everyone will be salted with fire',* it means that no one can escape the salt and the fire. But those who have welcomed the spirit into themselves and worked with it will be salted with the fire of life, whereas those who have gone against the spirit will be salted with the fire of suffering and death. It is sad, but this law is impossible to escape.

You'll say, 'But if we know how to preserve and increase the salt in ourselves, does that mean we never suffer?' No, of course we suffer, because on earth it is impossible to escape suffering. But it's not the same kind of suffering. The suffering that comes from the loss of your salt is terrible, for you have opened yourself to death, and once death is inside you, what weapons will you have to fight with to regain the upper hand? But if you have learned to preserve your salt, suffering will become a blessing for you, because you will know how to use it to grow and become clearer in yourself.

Notes
1. See *'You are Gods'*, part V, chap. 3: 'Evil can be compared to tenants'.
2. See *Angels and Other Mysteries of The Tree of Life,* Izvor 236, chap. 3: 'The angelic hierarchies'.

3. See *'Know Thyself' (part 1)*, CW 17, chap. 3, III: 'Spirit and matter'.
4. See *Sons and Daughters of God*, Izvor 240, chap. 1: 'I came that they may have life' and chap. 4: 'Leave the dead to bury their own dead'.
5. See *'Et il me montra un fleuve d'eau de la vie'*, part VI, chap. 1: 'L'écran de la conscience', p.198.
6. See *What is a Spiritual Master?*, Izvor 207.
7. See *The Splendour of Tiphareth*, CW 10, chap. 21.

Chapter Five

TASTING THE FLAVOUR OF THE SALT:
DIVINE LOVE

When I see so many fine young girls and boys in the world, so full of life and spontaneity, I want to say to them, 'Preserve for as long as possible your soul's freshness and the light in your expression. You don't know yet how precious that all is. It's a flavour, a salt that will enable you to win the love of the whole world. Everyone will love you and seek you out.' But at the same time, I must reproach adults in the strongest terms for not realizing the harm they cause adolescents when they expose them to all the temptations of materialism and sexuality.[1]

We often hear criticisms like 'Look what the young are interested in these days! Look what they read... what they listen to... how they entertain themselves!' But who creates and makes available all these useless, frivolous, even danger things they are attracted to? It's adults, isn't it?

people are fourteen or fifteen years ol

is social and material success held

ideal, but it is considered natural, e

them to have all sorts of sexual e

films, radio, television, music, etc, all encourage them
to seek adventures that will age them prematurely and
turn them into dull, prosaic, cynical beings with no
ideals. At which point, the very people who led them
along this path no longer find them as charming, so
they reject them and replace them with others who
are purer, for whom they reserve the same fate.

Adults seek out young people; they love young
people and enjoy their freshness and innocence, but
they don't rest until they've destroyed it. And when
these poor boys and girls eventually realize they
have lost everything, they are so disillusioned and
unhappy! The truth is that this situation is no good
for anyone, either for the young or for the adults. And
there is only one solution: that we all learn what we
must look for in each other so we can love and be
loved, that we each strive to discover the flavour, the
salt, that makes people so precious and allows them
to sense what makes *all* creatures precious. You see,
the subject of salt is a far-reaching one.

People think they know what it is they love about
a particular man or woman – their beauty, their charm
or their moral or intellectual qualities, and so on. In
reality, we only ever love the One, the Creator, who
made these beings what they are. Yes, it is the Creator
you love through all creatures. The more the divine
manifests in them as goodness, wisdom, beauty, light
and strength, the more you love them. The divine is
this salt that gives them flavour. This is why, in spite
of your efforts, you will never find fulfilment and

perfect joy if you do not seek a vaster, richer reality in the person you love. Very soon you will have explored everything about them and will become bored and disappointed. Then you will look for another love, but, again, very soon the same boredom and disappointment will return. All your objections and all your efforts will change nothing. As long as you fail to seek the Divinity in the person you love, you will never know fulfilment, because you will be on the wrong track.

Love the Creator, the One who is the source of all life, and you will feel him manifest through every creature. It is he, the One, whom you will love in them, and your heart and soul will find what they are looking for. We have accounts of the amorous affairs and conquests of numerous men and women throughout history who did not understand this truth and suffered tragic fates. The beings of flesh and blood you claim to love or be looking for are only intermediaries, conduits destined to transmit divine energy, and if you want to continue to love them, you must remember, every day, to re-establish contact with the higher world.[2]

Don't worry, then, about needing to know who it is you ought to love or who it is you hope will love you. Love God above all, and he will appear before you through his creatures, smiling upon you and filling you with joy. You will love them and be loved by them, because you will love the Divinity that dwells in them and because they too will discover the Divinity through you.

Those who turn away from God, who cut their connection with him, allow the source of love in themselves to run dry, and one day, faced with the successive failures of their love life, they will ask themselves how they could have loved all these people so much. On first meeting they had seemed irresistible, but gradually they had begun to find them perfectly ordinary or even unbearable. This is quite simply because the unique Being who had dwelt in any particular man or woman was no longer there for them. It wasn't him or her they loved, but the Being that looked out at them from their loved one, and they didn't know how to do what was needed to hold onto this Being. They were careless, thoughtless and egotistical, and the Being living in this man or woman withdrew.

So do not seek out men and women for themselves but in order to discover in them the unique Being who will visit you through them. And then all those close to you and around you will become sources of constant joy, because the unique Being will not abandon you. Wherever you go, God will come and manifest himself; you will feel him, you will taste him. You may leave your country, go anywhere, and you will meet him endlessly and everywhere through others. But the day you break your link with him, do not count on anyone giving you this flavour.

If you forget where your blessings come from, your source will eventually run dry. It would be like stopping at a fountain, thinking it was the water source itself. You draw water from it and drink it as if it should last forever. And yet all it takes is for someone to divert the current that feeds the fountain for the water to stop flowing and the fountain to no longer give you anything. Stay linked therefore to the primordial Source, for it will never cease pouring its waters into you – the waters of joy.[3]

Love… There is nothing humans need more, but there is nothing they feel so uncertain about. One day a young man visited me; he told me he was engaged, that he loved his fiancée and was sure she loved him, but all the same he was asking himself certain questions. He had difficulty expressing what he was feeling and eventually said, 'When I look deep into my fiancée's eyes, I don't really know who I'm looking at, and I don't know what in me is looking at her either.' I was struck by the subtlety of this comment, for it is true: people's identity is a great mystery. What are the entities that inhabit us and also inhabit our family members, our friends and all those around us? We do not know. In fact, each of us is a dwelling-place, which a succession of different kinds of spirits comes to occupy, and really it's impossible to know who exactly we have before us.

So I said to this young boy, 'I can explain it to you like this. The young girl you love is inhabited by entities that give her what it is you love about her. So ask God not to allow these entities to leave either her or you, because then you would lose your love. And also pray that those entities that inhabit you and make her love you do not leave you either.' I sensed he was listening to me very carefully, and he left deep in thought. Well, that gives you something to think about as well, doesn't it?

Notes
1. See Youth: *Creators of the Future,* Izvor 233, chap. 18: 'Sexual freedom' and chap. 19: 'Preserve the poetry of your love'.
2. See *The Seeds of Happiness,* Izvor 231, chap. 20: 'Fusion on the higher planes'.
3. See *'Cherchez le Royaume de Dieu et sa Justice',* part VIII, chap. 2, III: 'À la source divine de l'amour'.

Chapter Six

'YOU ARE THE LIGHT OF THE WORLD'

Never accept the materialist philosophy of 'facts', which encourages the majority to say, 'That's how things are, that's the situation, it's perfectly clear and obvious, nothing can be done about it'. And you must also reject all the rationalizations and logical arguments you use to attribute natural causes to your weaknesses and thus justify them: 'That's how I am, it's my nature, and you can't fight nature'.

Likewise, if an illness shows itself and tries to gain a foothold in you, try to resist it. Even if you are already ill, try to maintain the notion that you are healthy, for even in a body that's sick there are always a few healthy cells that can save the others. If every healthy cell succeeds in rallying a few sick cells to its credo, your whole body will gradually recover. On the other hand, if the last remaining healthy cells adopt the point of view of their sick neighbours, you've had it.

All it takes is for at least one healthy atom in your body to convince the others, by assuring them and demonstrating to them that anything is possible, even the impossible! By strength of spirit, then, refuse to accept all evidence of illness, of weakness, of difficult situations, of failure… With this attitude you will save at least one atom, whose influence will eventually win over all the others.

Those who do not grasp this truth or who refuse to put it into practice will always be prey to weaknesses, limitations and illness. Magic, which is the science of the power of the spirit, always looks beyond certain evidence. When a white mage is ill, they say, 'My body is ill, it is true, but I am a son of God, a divine spark, and as such can be neither ill, nor extinguished, nor weak.' And this belief places them above their illness. They identify not with their body but with their spirit, which lives in the light and in eternity.

So, take the decision to introduce this truth into your life, even if it seems impossible at first. Human beings now cling so habitually to what they call evidence! Some say, 'I'm ill, you can see for yourself, and no one can tell me otherwise.' But what they don't know is that by affirming their illness in this way they reinforce it. Yes, they are ill, but the way they admit it takes away from their ability to react. Although the illness only affects one part of their body, they identify with it and allow it to occupy their whole mind.

As for people who think it's good to go around predicting disasters, based on their observations of other people's mistakes and anomalies, their attitude is contributing to any disasters that do occur. They can then say, 'I told you so!' Knowing the facts, they would have been better advised to find ways of remedying the situation. For there are always solutions, and even if they are not sufficient to correct everything, they can at least prevent the worst.

So try to imprint this truth on your mind – that the spirit can triumph over everything. Believe me, you must not surrender in the face of evidence, for to surrender is to limit yourself. Those who succumb in the face of evidence make slaves of themselves, whereas those who bring forward the powers of the spirit in all circumstances exercise their thinking, struggle, progress and become master of all situations. And eventually, one after the other, the obstacles fall away.

When you decide to apply the law of the pre-eminence of the spirit in your life, the first changes you create are in the realm of thought. These changes then influence the realm of feelings, sensations and emotions, where gradually everything becomes lighter and more fluid. And finally, these changes materialize on the physical plane, where things become clear and organized.[1]

We will not live on the earth or in our physical body for all eternity. This is why, in our psychic and spiritual life, we must never bow to the evidence the physical world presents us with. Rather, we must always seek ways for the spirit to triumph. Matter, with all the obstacles it presents, is given to us as a stimulus for the spirit, and by 'matter' I mean not only the physical world but also the psychic world, which is also matter – matter that is less opaque than the physical world's, but matter all the same. So you must no longer say, 'There's nothing I can do, it's plain to see, there's this and I feel that…' By stating what is real, you think it proves you right, since it *is* real, but there are other realities that elude you. You capitulate when faced with material, objective reality, but if you know how to act there is another reality, equally evident, that will have the final word: divine Reality.

I am opening a door for you to the light. I am showing you the path to powers you can put to work in your inner struggles. Commit yourself to this new direction, and gradually, with time, you will triumph. If you have understood me properly, you will realize that it only remains for you to go forward, and no one will be able to stop you.

A long time ago, the Master Peter Deunov gave us this formula: *'God is light within me, the angels are warmth, human beings are kindness'*, to be said three times. Then: *'God is light within me, my spirit is warmth, and I am kindness'*, also to be said three times. These formulas are affirmations. 'I am kindness.' Yes, even a wicked person will eventually become good if he repeats these words with conviction and with the sincere wish to improve. These formulas from the Master Peter Deunov recall certain sayings from Jesus which are also powerful affirmations: *'The Father and I are one'*,[2] *'My Father is still working, and I also am working'*,[3] *'I am the resurrection and the life'*,[4] *'I am the light of the world.'*

When Jesus says, *'I am the light of the world'*, he is identifying with the sun. Indeed, what is the light of the world if not the sun, the visible, dazzling image of the Divinity? And when we identify, it means we recognize we are something other than what is revealed by our physical appearance, that we possess another nature, that we are made of another quintessence, which we decide to let take our place.

For Jesus to have been able to say *'I am the light of the world'* and to have found this light in himself and risen within to meet it, he must have succeeded in identifying with the spiritual sun, the Christ. And this is true love: the irresistible force which drives people to seek what is purest and most divine in themselves and, when they have found it, to merge with this reality. Yes, this attraction is what love is; God has placed a spark within the soul of human beings, creating the need for them to find him again and to become one with him.

Humans will not know or understand anything of God unless they feel him within themselves as life, power, love and light. True revelation is found in the sensation and the certainty that the Lord is within us and we are fused with him, that there is no separation between him and us.

All these phrases Jesus said represent the goal we must also attain if we are to become true sons and daughters of God. There is no point in claiming to be a Christian, a disciple of Christ, if we do not work to realize what Jesus himself realized and was able to claim: *'My Father is still working, and I also am working', 'The Father and I are one', 'I am the resurrection and the life', 'I am the light of the world'.* It's not me telling you this; it's Jesus. But have you read the Gospels properly?

Yes, *'You are the salt of the earth'*, asserted Jesus to the crowd following him on the mountain, and *'You are the light of the world'.* What he said to them was also said for us. Light is the celestial fire, and salt is a manifestation of this light. If, from this spark – your spirit, which lives within you – you succeed little by little in illuminating your whole being, not only will you become the salt that vitalizes the earth and gives it flavour, but you will possess the same powers and bring the same blessings as the light.

Of course, anyone can claim *'I am the light of the world',* but if you have not already done the work that gives you the right to say such a phrase, you will expose yourself to great dangers, and people will be forced to lock you up somewhere. Oh yes, many people who are so-called 'mad' doubtless possess an intuition of their true divine nature, but it is not enough to have this intuition and advertise it. You must also seek to make it a reality and, meanwhile, remain humble and work.

'You are the salt of the earth', 'You are the light of the world' – these truths represent the highest ideal one can attain. Never doubt them, but at the same time make sure you adapt them to your life on earth, to your human condition. Whatever your spiritual ideal, never forget that you are part of the physical

world. It is all very well to reject the evidence-based materialist philosophy, but you must also bear in mind that you live on the physical plane. Yes, because the physical plane opposes and resists us; it persists in contradicting us and has brought down many great, powerful, formidable men and women! The physical plane doesn't give in easily; it obeys only when we attack it with powerful blows, with means as physical as its own, since physical force is all it understands. This is how it reasons: 'What you say about the power of the spirit is very true, but this has nothing to do with my world. Only the powers of matter can affect me.'

We are forced to admit that the physical plane knows and recognizes only our physical body, that is to say, what we can do with the muscles of our arms and legs, or with tools and machines. It isn't impressed with our psychological and spiritual faculties. So we must reconcile the realities of the physical plane with the assertion that we can reject material evidence and subscribe to the school of true force, the school of light, the school of the spirit, since spirit and matter co-exist. And it is precisely this that Christians stubbornly reject in their conception of Jesus.

Of course, Jesus declared himself to be not only *'the light of the world'* but also *'the living bread that came down from heaven'* and *'the way, and the truth, and the life.'*[5] And he also said, *'I am the gate. Whoever enters by me will be saved.'* Yet he was unable to escape the demands of the physical plane: he got hungry, thirsty and tired. And he was vulnerable, as shown in certain passages in the Gospels, which mention that he had to flee to escape the Pharisees, who wanted to stone him. And when the end came, he felt all the agony of death. Jesus is able to serve as such an example for us, precisely because he was made of matter and spirit, as we are, and knew how to reconcile the two. If he had been 'the Son of God' in the sense that Christians understand it, in other words God himself, the second person of the Trinity, the Christ, and not a human being, how would we be able to take him as our model? His essence would be different from ours.[6]

Jesus also said, *'Be perfect, therefore, as your heavenly Father is perfect',*[7] in order to teach us not to yield in the face of what we call human weakness. But now it is up to us, in our own lives, not to confuse the world of matter and the world of spirit, to give each its own place, while always giving pre-eminence to the spirit, to the light.

Try, therefore, to acquire a taste for working with the light, not only sunlight but also that invisible light which permeates the whole of creation,[8] for light alone is capable of re-establishing order within us, of making all our cells vibrate in harmony and of restoring our health. But who thinks of light as being the most powerful remedy? It may not be the quickest, but its effects are permanent.

More than anything else in your life, think of the light, for its vibrations are so extremely subtle that it brings us close to the world of spirit. For at least a few minutes each day, think only of the light and nothing else. It will be like a beam of pure, powerful particles, passing through you to reach all creatures on earth and awaken their divine nature.

Concentration on light is the true salvation, because God is light. When you think of light, you link yourself to him. When Jesus said, *'I am the light of the world',* this meant 'The Father is in me and I am in the Father'. But he also told us, *'You are the light of the world.'* It is worth reflecting on this capacity for identification that's been given to us.[9] Physically we have a certain appearance, which allows others to recognize us: there is no mistaking certain physical forms. But inwardly we have the ability to identify with everything that exists, and this is what we actually do, more or less unconsciously, throughout the day. Something in us never ceases to identify by imitation with what we touch, see and hear. So it pays to be vigilant!

Every day we must stop for a few moments and ask ourselves who and what we are identifying with, because the people and things we identify with are what we will become, sooner or later. And since Jesus said, *'You are the light of the world',* what we must identify with is light, so that one day we will really become light.

Notes

1. See *'Cherchez le Royaume de Dieu et sa Justice',* part II, chap. 4: 'Du soleil à la terre: comment la pensée se réalise dans la matière'.

2. See above, part VII: 'Mon père travaille et moi aussi je travaille avec Lui'.
3. See *'You are Gods'*, part I, chap. 2: 'The Father and I are one'.
4. See *La Fête de Pâques – 'Je suis la résurrection et la vie'*, brochure 308.
5. See *'Et il me montra un fleuve d'eau de la vie'*, part VII, chap. 5: 'Je suis le chemin, la vérité et la vie'.
6. See *Sons and Daughters of God,* Izvor 240, chap. 7: 'The man Jesus and the cosmic Principle of the Christ'.
7. See *'You are Gods'*, part I, chap. 1: 'Be perfect as your heavenly Father is perfect'.
8. See above, part III, chap. 2: 'The Tree of Life', pp. 159-162.
9. See *'Et il me montra un fleuve d'eau de la vie'*, part VI, chap. 4: 'L'identification, un changement d'état de conscience'.

Chapter Seven

THE ALCHEMISTS' SALT

Nutrition is an inexhaustible topic, and I continue to draw your attention in all kinds of ways to the daily activity of eating, so vital to all creatures. I have often likened nutrition to a love letter sent by the Creator that we must learn to decipher.[1] When food arrives on our table to bring us life, health and joy, it already has an entire history. The four elements have contributed to its formation, and now it speaks to us of the earth, of water, of the air and the sun but also of the entities that have been busy since time immemorial infusing it with their particular properties and virtues.

Salt plays a part in our diet every day. It seems quite natural to put it on the table along with the water and bread. But so many events have marked the history of salt since it first appeared in the primitive ocean that our earth gradually emerged from! Salt is inseparable from our origins, and we have a vital need for it. Not only does it flavour our food, it also preserves it. But do you think about this when you put salt in the food you are cooking or on your plate?

You have a little taste to see whether there is enough, and your tongue responds while your head is off somewhere else.

But don't you think this is just the time to be deciphering the letter God is sending you through the intermediary of salt? What a long road it has travelled, coming from the sea, being dried by the sun's rays and finally arriving at your table! And now that it's about to become part of you, it is also important to explore its symbolic meaning by meditating on the words of Jesus: *'You are the salt of the earth.'*

In another passage in the Gospels, Jesus also says, *'Have salt in yourselves and be at peace with one another.'* What is the connection between salt and the peace that must reign among human beings? I mentioned to you that in certain countries salt is offered with bread as a sign of welcome. This gesture implicitly refers to the harmonious relations that men and women must establish with one another when they eat together. We don't sit down at the same table in order to squabble – even if this happens! Eating together is generally considered a sign of friendship. When we feel affection and friendship for someone, straightaway we think of inviting them for a meal.

What is this salt inside us, then, that allows us to live in peace with one another? In one of his talks, the Master Peter Deunov said, 'It is only by means of salt, by means of this balance between your head and your heart, that you will restore peace within yourself and understand the divine world.' In order to understand what this salt is that represents the balance between head and heart, we must consult chemistry and even alchemy.

Chemistry defines salt as the product created when an acid acts on a base. Acid, which is an active, dynamic substance, can be likened to the masculine principle, and the base, which is a passive, receptive substance, can be likened to the feminine principle. In the presence of an acid, a base reacts to produce a salt. This salt, then, is the child, the fruit, of the acid father and base mother.

Father, mother and child – here we have the first family unit. Whether on the physical, psychic or spiritual plane, all manifestation is based on three principles, the first two giving birth to the third. This model is a repetition of the original model, in which the two great cosmic principles – masculine, the heavenly Father, and feminine, the divine Mother – unite in order to create. Everything that exists is the outcome of the union of these two principles. Every manifestation in the universe is the result of an encounter between a masculine and a feminine principle.

Using this model of father, mother and child, we can form other families: wisdom, love and truth; head, heart and will; thought, feeling and action; light, heat and movement; acid, base and salt.[2] In effect, truth is the child of wisdom and love, the will is the child of the head and the heart, action the child of thought and feeling, movement the child of light and heat, and salt the child of an acid and a base. This same family can be found in alchemy in the form of sulphur, mercury and salt.

Alchemists, then, like chemists, work with an element they call salt. Yes, but what they call salt has nothing in common with the chemical substance of the same name, and the same is true for mercury and sulphur. It is only their relationship that is identical: just as salt in chemistry is the product of an acid on a base, so in alchemy it is the product of sulphur and mercury.

By sulphur, then, we are meant to understand the masculine principle, which manifests in us as mind and spirit, and by mercury the feminine principle, which manifests as heart and soul. And salt, meaning the will, represents the balance which ideally reigns between the two. The will is expressed through action, and it is through their actions that human beings reveal the degree to which they have been able to create harmony between their mind and heart, between their thoughts and feelings. Through their physical body they express the riches of their spirit and soul, whose instruments are the mind and heart. By means of their physical body, which is the instrument of their will, they must bring the divine into the world.

At the end of the Emerald Tablet, Hermes Trismegistus says, 'This is why I have been called Hermes Trismegistus – that is to say 'three times very great' – since I possess the three parts of the universal Science.' Universal Science is the science of the three worlds: the divine world (we can also call it the 'spiritual world', meaning spiritual in the highest sense), the psychic world and the physical world. Alchemists work in the third world, the physical world, that of concretization, materialization.

If we divide the four sciences – alchemy, astrology, magic and the Cabbalah – among the three worlds – physical, psychic and spiritual – we could say that alchemy corresponds to the physical world, astrology and magic to the psychic world, and the Cabbalah to the spiritual world. These four sciences can also be related to our own organism.

The Cabbalah, which is the study of the world of principles, of numbers, corresponds to the brain.

Astrology corresponds to the heart and lungs, and magic to the hands. Astrology is the study of influences, of the currents of energy circulating in the universe, just as blood and air circulate in our body. And magic is the study of methods of working with these currents. The psychic world, in effect, is made up of two regions, which represent what initiatic Science calls the soul. Remember what I told you about the soul – that it is made up of two regions (the mental plane and the astral plane) and constitutes a pathway for the transformation and passage of energies between the spirit and the body.[3] *(See shema p. 132)*

Finally, alchemy, the study of the art of trans-forming matter, corresponds to the stomach, the organ in which materials accumulate before being elaborated.

The science of alchemy is therefore based on three principles: sulphur, mercury and salt... But since these are not to be confused with the chemical substances of the same name, what exactly are they? Alchemists explain their origin in the following way: fire, acting on air, formed sulphur; air, acting on water, formed mercury, and water, acting on earth, formed salt. And each one is represented by a symbol: ♐ sulphur, mercury ☿ and salt ⊕.

But here again, the fire, air, water and earth I'm speaking of are not the same as the ones we generally refer to as the four elements. In order to understand what they represent, we must refer to what the Cabbalists teach when they speak of the Hayot haKodesch, the four Holy Living Creatures, the entities located at the top of the angelic hierarchy, which sing continually day and night before the throne of God, *'Holy, holy, holy, is the Lord God Almighty, who was and is and is to come.'*[4] These four Holy Living Creatures – the Lion, which corresponds to fire; Man, who corresponds to air; the Eagle, which corresponds to water, and the Bull, which corresponds to earth – represent the quintessence of matter as it appears in its original purity. According to the alchemists, it is these four original elements which formed what they call sulphur, mercury and salt, by acting upon one another. Salt is therefore the endpoint of an entire process of condensation from fire to earth.

But you will never encounter the alchemists' sulphur, mercury and salt in nature, since they do not exist in matter. They represent principles acting within creation. This is why sulphur, the masculine principle, can designate fire, or the spirit, or the mind; and mercury, the feminine principle, can designate water, or the soul, or the heart. As for salt, it represents the fruit of their union. In order to express this idea, the alchemists used the figure of the equilateral triangle. And, if you remember, this is also the figure I used in my first talk* to explain the structure of the human psyche.

This figure is the symbol for the balance which reigns within us between the three principles when they have been equally and harmoniously developed. Now you understand why the Master Peter Deunov calls salt the balance between heart and mind. And

* 'The second birth', Paris, 29 January, 1938

you also understand Jesus' words, *'Have salt in yourselves, and be at peace with one another.'* When we have this salt, as a result of the harmony between the two principles of mind and heart, then balance, harmony and peace will be established within us, and we will also be at peace with one another.

How can humans ever be at peace with one another when, within themselves, there are absolute battlefields?[5] Everything worth experiencing obeys the laws of harmony.[6] The entire science and all the powers of the initiates are based on harmony. And this harmony, which rests on an equilibrium between the two principles, must begin with humans themselves. Only then will the salad be a success!

You are obviously surprised that now I'm talking to you about salad. Well, you wouldn't be, if you paid more attention to what you put on your plates, as I was saying to you earlier. The vegetables we call 'salad' would taste bland if we didn't season them with a dressing, which generally consists of oil, vinegar and salt. The mildness of the oil reduces the vinegar's acidity, and the salt enhances and harmonizes their flavours. Here again we discover a correspondence between these elements and our inner life, and I will leave you to meditate on this theme as well.

Notes
1. See *The Yoga of Nutrition,* Izvor 204, chap. 3: 'Food: a love-letter from God'.
2. See *The Second Birth,* CW 1.

3. See *'Et il me montra un fleuve d'eau de la vie'*, part III, chap. 2: 'Sur la nature de l'âme'.
4. See *The Book of Revelations: a Commentary*, Izvor 230, chap. 7: 'The twenty-four elders and the four holy living creatures'.
5. See *The Egregor of the Dove or the Reign of Peace*, Izvor 208.
6. See *Harmony and Health*, Izvor 225.

Chapter Eight

'AND AS ALL THINGS ARE ONE
AND COME FROM THE ONE'

Thus, the sulphur and mercury used in alchemy represent the two creative principles, masculine and feminine, active in the universe and within the human being, and salt is the result of this action. We therefore need to consider these three substances – sulphur, mercury and salt – as symbols of the psychic factors we have to work with.

You will say, 'But this isn't our idea of alchemy! We've always read and heard that the people who practised it were looking for the secret of how to turn metals into gold.' This is true, but alchemy is also something quite different, and turning metals into gold is only a secondary and limited aspect. Alchemy is the art of transforming matter – physical matter and, especially, psychic matter.[1] This is why, before they go diving into books on alchemy which they won't understand and, more importantly, rushing into experiments which will come to nothing, all those who are curious about this science should begin by studying the philosophical principles on which it is based. And the first of these principles is the unity of matter.

When we open our eyes on the world, what strikes us first is its richness and diversity. Life manifests through such different expressions, forms, colours and movements! And yet this diversity has as its origin a single essence: the divine emanation.[2] The universe was formed by successive condensations and differentiations, as it says in the Emerald Tablet, where the principles of alchemy are set out: 'And as all things are one and come from the One, through the meditation of the One*, all things are born of one thing through adaptation.' And it is because the universe is made from a single substance that, within this substance, passage from one state to another, from one form to another, is possible.

This single substance – the primordial matter which is the source of all forms of life – is called 'chaos' by the alchemists. And chaos is the abyss mentioned in the first verses of *Genesis: 'In the beginning God created the heavens and the earth. The earth was without form and void, and darkness was upon the face of the deep; and the Spirit of God was moving over the face of the waters. And God said, "Let there be light"; and there was light.'* Before God called on the light, only darkness existed. Yes, God caused the light to shine forth from out of the darkness. The alchemists understood this and entitled one of their treatises 'Light emerging by itself from the darkness'. Light is a projection of the darkness. From time to time, out of this original

* or 'through the mediation of the One' in other versions

darkness, centres of light suddenly appear, the cosmic phenomena known as nebulae and galaxies, which today's astronomers and astrophysicists continue to explore.

'...And the spirit of God was moving over the face of the waters.' I have already explained to you on several occasions why water is comparable to matter, in contrast to fire, which is comparable to spirit.[3]

When we speak of water, we instantly think of the liquid expanses we encounter in nature – rivers, lakes and seas, for example – which are channelled and eventually arrive in our houses to be put to different uses. But in nature, water is not necessarily visible. It is present everywhere in the atmosphere in the form of humidity and, through condensation, then becomes steam, mist, clouds and fog, until finally it falls as drops of rain. Under the effects of cold, it can solidify into ice, becoming so hard it can burst pipes, break up rocks and bring ocean liners to a halt. And when water falls from the sky, it can take the form not only of raindrops but also of delicate snowflakes, or of hailstones capable of knocking people out and destroying crops and the roofs of houses.

Yes, water is a multi-faceted element that enables us to understand, by analogy, how the same original substance passes alternately through different states, becoming either denser or more subtle. In the same way, our physical body, our soul and our spirit are merely different manifestations of a single substance. There is no real break between them. But of course the

link between them is not a direct one; passage from
one to another takes place by way of the different
subtle bodies, from the etheric to the atmic.

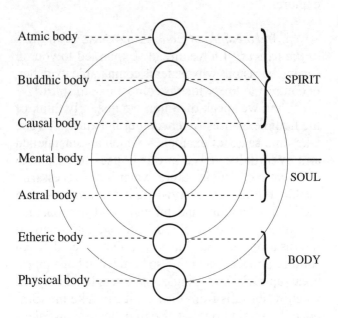

    What a difference there is between steam and ice!
And yet we're talking about the same substance. And
what a difference between the spirit and the physical
body! There would seem to be no relationship
between the two. And yet there is: the matter of
the physical body has its origin in the spirit, and, in
keeping with the analogy with water, we could say
that it condensed and hardened through 'cooling'.
And when Hermes Trismegistus declares at the

end of the Emerald Tablet, 'I am called Hermes Trismegistus, because I possess knowledge of the three worlds', he reveals the continuity that exists between the different planes of the universe, in other words, the unity of creation.

If we now study water from the point of view of chemistry, we see it is made from a combination of two gasses, which fuse under the effect of an electric spark. The formula for water is H_2O, which means that a molecule of water is composed of two atoms of hydrogen and one atom of oxygen. So hydrogen is 2, the number of the feminine principle, and oxygen is 1, the number of the masculine principle. Thus, water is the child of an oxygen father and a hydrogen mother. Is it possible to understand this mystery, whereby two gasses, representing the element of air, come together to produce a liquid? Two gasses, symbols of the masculine and feminine principles, united by the fire of love, give birth to water.[4] In comparison to the subtle matter of these gasses from which water is formed, water itself is quite concrete and material, and it is water which brings us life.

The different forms in which water appears give us an idea, then, of the different states through which psychic and physical matter pass, from the densest to the subtlest. Fire (the spirit) is all-powerful in relation to water (or matter), but just as with water, we must understand fire on the different planes – physical, psychic and spiritual. So the work we have to do in our inner life can also be symbolized as the work of fire on water. Heated by the fire of the spirit, the matter within us becomes more and more pure, more and more subtle.

Well then, what practical applications for our inner life can we draw from this knowledge of fire and water? There are many, but here is just one: since fire is all-powerful in relation to water, it is possible to shrink the psychic tumours formed by the accumulation of our negative states by changing our inner matter (water) into a state of vapour by means of fire (spirit).

Basically, the only subject of study for true mages and true alchemists is fire and water, for which air and earth serve merely as receptacles, as the Emerald Tablet again says, concerning the spirit: 'The sun is its father, the moon its mother, the wind carried it in its belly and the earth is its nurse.' Here the sun represents fire, and the moon water. Then Hermes Trismegistus adds, 'The father of all things, the *telesma* of the world, is here; its power remains intact if it is converted into earth.' Which means that the power of the spirit can act in even the densest matter, as represented by the earth element.

Every person and every object can be impregnated by this *telesma,* this force derived from the sun.[5] When introduced into objects, it is this force that makes talismans of them. And it is this same force that we are able to harness and accumulate within us when we go to contemplate the sunrise. In this work, our whole being – spirit, soul, mind and heart – is mobilized, so that our physical body may become the receptacle of this solar force, this symbol of the Divinity.

Water contains even greater mysteries, and these mysteries are related to blood. Blood is sublimated water. There are great analogies between water and blood, and not just between water and blood but between water, blood and light. The sun's light, which is its blood, is also a higher form of water. This is why Christ said, *'Those who eat my flesh and drink my blood have eternal life.'*[6] This blood is the light that comes from the sun.

Because water is part of your everyday life, you think you know it. No, you know only a few aspects of it and a few uses for it. When you are able to experience water as blood and light and think of it as such, then, and only then, will you know it.

Notes

1. See *True Alchemy or the Quest for Perfection,* Izvor 221.
2. See *'Et il me montra un fleuve d'eau de la vie',* part II, chap. 1: 'L'engendrement des mondes'.
3. See *'Cherchez le Royaume de Dieu et sa Justice',* part II, chap. 1, I: 'Et l'esprit de Dieu se mouvait au-dessus des eaux'.
4. See *Langage symbolique, langage de la nature,* OC 8, chap. VIII: 'Le vrai mariage'.
5. See *The Splendour of Tiphareth,* CW 10, chap. 14: 'The sun has the solution to the problem of love – telesma'.
6. See *'Cherchez le Royaume de Dieu et sa Justice',* part VI, chap. 2, III: 'Celui qui mange ma chair et qui boit mon sang a la vie éternelle'.

Chapter Nine

THE WORK OF THE ALCHEMIST:
3 OVER 4

In concentrating their effort on transforming matter, alchemists gained a better understanding of spiritual work than many so-called spiritual people who strive to escape matter and keep body and spirit separate. Alchemy does not split the human being in half, into a spirit which alone is worthy of our attention and a body which should be ignored, despised and mistreated. Spirit and matter, spirit and body, have work to do together. The body is not a grave for the spirit. Or, more precisely, the body is a grave for the spirit only for those who haven't understood the meaning of the first verse in the book of *Genesis: 'In the beginning God created the heavens and the earth.'*[1] Yes, not just the heavens, but the heavens and the earth. 'Heavens' should be taken to mean spirit and 'earth' to mean matter, and since God created them both they must have something to do together.

Separating the body from the spirit is like separating a house from its roof: when the house is exposed to bad weather, it disintegrates. And how can you have a roof without four walls to support it?

Let's stay with the image of the house. Schematically, a house is a square with a triangle on top. The triangle is above the square, 3 over 4. The 3 stands for the three principles – mind, heart and will – through which the Holy Trinity – Father, Son and Holy Spirit – expresses itself in us, and so it represents the spiritual world. And the 4 stands for the four elements (or the four states of matter) and the four directions in space, in other words the physical world.

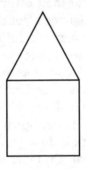

As we have seen, these three principles and four elements are what alchemists based their science and their work on. The three principles are sulphur, mercury and salt; the four elements are earth, water, air and fire. When we add 3 and 4 together, we arrive at 7, which symbolizes the union of spirit and matter.

When you reflect on matter, you inevitably think of dimensions and space. Space is not something vague and undefined; it conforms to a structure which corresponds to the number 4 – the four cardinal points. And human beings, as microcosms created in the image of the macrocosm, are also, in a way, constructed according to the number 4. With their arms stretched out to the side, forming a horizontal line, which crosses the vertical line running from head to feet, they replicate the directions in space.

'But what about the head?' you'll ask. 'Is it north, or is it east?' It doesn't really matter. The French say people have 'lost the north' when they lose control of their thoughts. But we can also say they are disorientated, and since the orient is the east, where the sun rises, east and north have the same meaning symbolically.

From another point of view, we can say that the head, which represents the spiritual part of a human being, corresponds to the number 3, which is above the 4 of the four limbs. So the head is the triangle, and as the triangle turns it generates a sphere. Why must it turn? It does so in order to maintain its balance; otherwise it would fall, the same way a spinning-top falls as soon as it stops spinning. Our head is placed on top to give us movement, for movement is the law of life, and this movement, this impulse, must always come from above.

But let's come back to the number 4, which represents the body of the house, with the roof, the number 3, placed on top. Yes, it's amazing; the house, the human being's dwelling-place, is there to remind us of the work the spirit ceaselessly carries out in matter. And this work, which is the very condition of life, must be achieved by each of us within ourselves, so we may become the dwelling-place of the Lord, or in the words of St. Paul, *'the temple of the living God'*.[2]

And now, let's leave two-dimensional space (the square and the triangle) and enter the three-dimensional space of the cube surmounted by the pyramid. The cube, which represents in terms of volume what the square does in terms of surface, is even more suited to representing the solidity and stability of matter on account of its compact shape. Yes, but matter owes its stability solely to the work of the spirit, which is symbolized by the pyramid, the four triangles that surmount the cube.[3] For matter

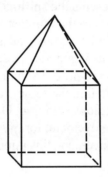

that is not animated and given life by the spirit disintegrates. The pyramid consists of four triangular faces, representing the two psychic principles (heart and mind) and the two spiritual principles (soul and spirit). Heart, mind, soul and spirit work on the matter of the physical body, or the cube.

To free yourself from the limitations of matter, you must leave the 4 behind and enter the 3, or the spirit. While you remain in matter, and look to matter for your development, fulfilment and salvation, it is not possible to leave your difficulties and weaknesses behind; you are restricted and imprisoned by them. Leaving the 4 behind and rising to the 3 is the only way out when suffering hardships. The 3, or the roof, is the place you must climb to, or where you must remain, whatever happens!

This is the meaning of Jesus' words: *'When you see the desolating sacrilege spoken of by Daniel the prophet, ... let him who is on the housetop not go down, nor enter his house, to take anything away.'* Do not go down from the housetop... Obviously what is recommended here must be understood as applying to the spiritual plane. For on the physical plane, what protection could you expect from a roof when you are in danger? Except of course in the case of flooding, when the water keeps rising. For anyone looking for physical shelter, it is better to go down to the cellar or to underground passages, which is what people sensibly do in times of war.

In the timeless language of symbols, the roof is the spirit, where one is always safe and at peace. So Jesus' advice concerns the psychic life. When trouble breaks out in the world or within you, you must never look below for help, but rather strive to rise as high as possible and remain at the summit, that is, reflect, reason and connect with heaven, in order to find peace and light. Only then can you see clearly and find the means to act, to save yourself and others too. People will often throw themselves into a fire, instead of running away from it! Why? Because they have 'gone down' from the roof, lost their head and allowed themselves to become overwhelmed by distress and emotion.

Jesus' advice is extremely valuable, as it concerns every aspect of our life. Whatever the physical or psychic dangers we may be exposed to, we have the greatest chance of saving ourselves if we remain on the roof, in other words in the spiritual world. There on high we discover precisely how we should act when we are in matter. We will never find salvation in matter; even the best material conditions can never protect us for all time. Why? Because if we no longer turn to the spirit to find the best way of using these conditions, they may even rebound on us.

You might say, 'Well, what should we do, then? Stay on the roof and desert the building below?' No, the two must never be separated. Since we have to live on earth in matter, we mustn't neglect either the cube or the pyramid but, rather, work on the cube from within the pyramid. It is then that we truly become a house, a dwelling-place, for the Lord and his angels. You must stop resembling a dwelling with no roof, for once the roof has been torn down you are left without protection.

Clearly, it is easier to come down from the roof than to climb up to it, and when you have succeeded in reaching it, it is difficult to stay up there. Coming down requires no effort: you only have to let yourself slide down – and it's so pleasant! Indeed it is, but you must nevertheless climb to the top and stay there, because that's where you will find pure air, light and freedom. We each have a cube, but why fill it with lead? In other words, why cling to matter at its densest, at its grossest? We should be filling the cube with gold, and to do so we must place the pyramid of the spirit above the cube.

Now let's take an image from astronomy. What does the roof represent in our universe? The sun. This is because it is at the centre and because, symbolically, the summit is identical to the centre. The centre and the periphery, or the summit and the base,

or the pyramid and the cube represent the two poles which we human beings endlessly oscillate between.[4] We mustn't stray from the centre and lose ourselves at the periphery.

And what is the periphery? It is all our distractions and all our so-called good reasons for abandoning that point right in the middle, where not only are we in control of our own life but we are able to assume our responsibilities towards other people, without favouring some over others. Every man and woman who has duties as a parent, teacher, instructor, company director or politician, etc., must find the

centre or summit, from where they will be able to
offer equal consideration and equal kindness to all
creatures. To contribute to the good of humanity,
you have to remain on the roof, above prejudices and
hasty judgment.

The numbers 3 and 4 speak to us of two worlds,
each governed by their own laws: the 3, the spirit,
is always in motion, and the 4, matter, is inert.
All life in the universe can be summed up by the
opposing energies of the numbers 3 and 4. Take
the zodiac, for example. The constellations form
an unchanging whole; they move through cosmic
space, but as one. No changes occur in the sequence,
no one constellation overtakes another: you won't
see Aquarius after Pisces or before Capricorn. The
planets, on the other hand, keep forming different
figures, in front of each other or behind each other,
or side by side. So you could say that the zodiac
represents the body and the planets the spirit.

In just the same way, the organs in our physical
body are in fixed positions, whereas the blood, fluids
and currents of energy within them keep circulating.
But it is thought, in particular, that has the capacity
for movement: it runs freely in all directions, with
limitless space opening out before it. In nature, as
in the human being, matter remains matter and spirit
spirit; we mustn't confuse the two but must learn
how each works on the other.

Spirit, 3, works on matter, 4. Together, 3 and 4
give us 7, which represents a living creature in whom

spirit and matter coexist harmoniously. The number 7 is one of the expressions of totality, as in the seven days of the week corresponding to the seven planets, the seven heavens and the seven colours, as well as the seven-stringed lyre, which symbolizes the seven bodies of the human being.[5] And if you take the six faces of the cube and add the four faces of the pyramid, 7 becomes 10, which is fulfilment.

You might say, 'But do we really learn anything from playing with numbers in this way?' Yes, definitely, since initiates have put a great deal of their science of numbers into certain games. Take the game of dice, for instance. On the different faces of a die there are dots representing the numbers 1 to 6, and their position is such that the sum of the dots on opposite faces is always 7. That's something else to think about: 6 and 7. And moreover, the die itself is a cube.

Beings and things can be studied from three perspectives: anatomical, physiological and psychological, corresponding to form (anatomy), content (physiology) and meaning (psychology). And this is also true for numbers. Most of the time we consider only the anatomical aspect of numbers, and because of the way we work with them they remain abstract, when in fact they are concrete, alive and meaningful. We see this when we shift from the anatomical to the physiological perspective to study the exchanges numbers make with each other. From the perspective of anatomy, $1 + 1 = 2$, but from the perspective of physiology $1 + 1 = 3$. However, to interpret numbers from the psychological perspective, we need to go even further, and again I'll give you an example for this.

In order to make their mark on matter, which is represented by the number 4 (as in the four elements), humans must rise to the 1. This submission of the 4 to the power of the 1, or spirit and will, is one meaning of the number 5. The 5 is the perfect human, symbolized by the pentagram: at the top, the head or spirit, governing the 4 (the four limbs and the four elements). 'And what about 6?' you might ask. The 6 corresponds to another reality. In fact, 6 is 2 x 3, and Solomon's seal, with its two interlaced inverted triangles, is based on this structure. The two triangles symbolize the

unity of matter and spirit in the universe, as well as the merging of the lower and higher natures in the human being. So Solomon's seal is a means of expressing the balance between antagonistic forces in the universe and in the human being, when matter is no longer in conflict with spirit, and our lower nature becomes the servant of our higher nature.[6]

When understood in this way, numbers become keys that open the door to all mysteries. But people are not used to seeing the deeper meaning of numbers, which is why so many passages in sacred texts remain obscure. The Cabbalists alone possess the true science of numbers.

As with the square surmounted by a triangle, the figure of the cubic stone surmounted by a pyramid (or 3 over 4) represents the spirit's work on matter, in other words the work of the two principles, the masculine (spirit) and the feminine (matter), which are the origin of all manifestation in the universe. In the language of the alchemists, these two principles are sulphur (the masculine principle) and mercury (the feminine principle), which together make salt.

So, then, the alchemists' salt relates to the cubic stone surmounted by a pyramid, and the cubic stone surmounted by a pyramid is a symbol for the philosopher's stone.

Notes

1. See *'Cherchez le Royaume de Dieu et sa Justice'*, part II, chap. 1: 'Au commencement Dieu créa le ciel et la terre'.
2. See above, part III: 'Vous êtes le temple du Dieu vivant'.
3. See *The Symbolic Language of Geometrical Figures,* Izvor 218, chap. 3: 'The triangle' and chap. 5: 'The pyramid'.
4. See *'Et il me montra un fleuve d'eau de la vie'*, part VI, chap. 2: 'Le travail sur le subconscient', pp. 211-213.
5. See above, part III, chap. 1: 'Le système des six corps'.
6. See *The Symbolic Language of Geometrical Figures*, Izvor 218, chap. 3: 'The triangle', part II.

Chapter Ten

THE PHILOSOPHER'S STONE,
FRUIT OF A MYSTIC UNION

The word 'alchemy' usually conjures up notions of mysterious knowledge and techniques which supposedly enabled certain figures in the past to make gold. But many other researchers, either eccentrics or charlatans, are said to have been caught up in experiments that left them exhausted and cost them all their possessions and sometimes even their mind. For in order to transmute metals into gold, they first had to obtain a certain substance with wonderful properties called 'the philosopher's stone', the preparation of which was an extremely long and complicated process.

Alchemists described the preparation of the philosopher's stone as 'woman's work and child's play'. But how can anyone who hasn't studied the great principles at work in the universe understand this phrase? In the first place, alchemists had the habit of revealing things and, at the same time, concealing them, making their treatises very difficult to understand: so, they reversed the order of the words, which should have read 'child's play and woman's work'. And what is this child's play? Is it marbles, tin soldiers, dolls?... And woman's work – is that housework, cooking, knitting?... Obviously not. What is meant here is a very particular kind of play and work, one that relates to the role and purpose of the masculine and feminine principles.

Woman's work is to carry a child in her womb and bring it into the world. The rest is not essential, even a man can do it. True woman's work is the work a man cannot do, whereas the 'child's play' is man's preserve. He does the 'playing' in order to give the woman the seed she will carry and bring to fruition. The game is short-lived, whereas woman's work takes much longer, lasting months on end.

So anyone wishing to penetrate the secret of the philosopher's stone must know the elements and processes set in motion when a man and a woman conceive a child, and then, when the child is conceived, must know how it is formed in its mother's womb. The preparation of the philosopher's stone obeys the same laws as those of conception and gestation, because the same laws govern the various kingdoms of creation.[1]

In alchemy, the masculine and feminine principles are sulphur and mercury, which unite to produce a child, salt. So we encounter the same cosmic process: the work of spirit on matter. Spirit fertilizes matter by introducing its quintessence into it, and the child born of this work is the entire universe with the myriad creatures populating it.

These days, the majority of chemists don't take alchemy seriously. At best they think of it as the forerunner of their science – a very primitive forerunner, of course, and completely outmoded. I won't enter into this debate, except to mention that one of the foundations of chemistry is the reaction: acid + base = salt (+ water), and that the philosopher's stone, which is the goal of alchemical work, is a salt formed by the union of sulphur and mercury. The acid represents the masculine principle, as does sulphur; the base represents the feminine principle, as does mercury, and in both cases their union forms a salt. Now, given that chemists and alchemists are not pursuing the same outcomes and aims, they have no reason to criticize each other or hold each other in contempt.

Alchemists describe the philosopher's stone as a red powder. Its essential properties are the capacity to transmute metals into silver or gold and ordinary stones into precious stones; to heal illness and prolong life and, finally, to reveal the secrets of nature. Through the course of history, emphasis has been placed mainly on the transmutation of metals, particularly lead, into gold. For a long time such research was considered to be the imagination of a few dreamers. But advances in nuclear physics have finally shown that such a transmutation is possible.

One atom of lead contains eighty-two electrons and eighty-two protons, whereas an atom of gold contains seventy-nine electrons and seventy-nine protons. So all it takes to transmute lead into gold is for the atomic structure of lead to be modified by removing three electrons, three protons and a few neutrons. Yes, this small change is all that is required. There have been some successful experiments carried out, but the cost of implementing them is so great that it's more worthwhile to carry on searching for gold in nature.

However, alchemists don't want to make do with what nature has to offer. The processes involved in the transformation of mineral matter in the bowels of the earth are extremely lengthy. The first deposits of gold or precious stones took millions of years to form! Alchemists seek to speed up these processes but also to 'improve' and 'perfect' matter by turning base metals into precious ones. And the secret of this improvement lies in the substance known as the philosopher's stone, the preparation of which has been, and still is, the object of so much research and experimentation.

The preparation of the philosopher's stone involves cooking a substance by placing it in a container known as 'philosopher's egg', which is then put into an oven called an *athanor*. But the alchemists do not state what temperature it should be cooked at. And, most importantly, although they call this substance by a great variety of names, they never say exactly what it is, except that it is made by bringing together a metal and a mineral. They claim that out of all the metals and minerals on earth, only one from each category can be combined together.

When the metal, which represents the masculine principle, and the mineral, the feminine principle, are put together in the crucible, they devour each other. A third substance then appears that is neither metal nor mineral but something that is unable to be broken down anymore. Here again alchemists conflict with chemists. When chemists combine a metal with a mineral, they are then able, with the help of certain procedures, to reverse the process and break down the resulting compound. But alchemists claim to know of a mineral and a metal which will devour each other to produce the basic matter from which the philosopher's stone can be extracted, and that this matter can no longer be broken down, as the compound is irreversible.

This theory becomes understandable and acceptable when transposed to a different domain. When a child comes into the world, it is as a result of the father and mother coming together. But how can you now 'break down' the child so that it reverts to its father on one side and its mother on the other? It's impossible. The child is a new entity, the product of a combination that cannot be reversed. The philosopher's stone is the child born of a mystic union.

For all its obscure elements, alchemy should not be disregarded as a science. On the contrary. If you take the trouble to look more deeply into the principles of alchemy, you will discover that all the matters it deals with are, in fact, vital to us. I told you that in participating in the transformation of matter the alchemist wishes to assist nature. Well, we too can assist nature in its efforts to transform us.

The preparation of the philosopher's stone is inscribed in the great book of life, and this book encompasses the universe as well as human beings. By working on our own matter, we can more rapidly become what we must become: the *'gold refined by fire'* mentioned in the book of *Revelations*. For it is fire that enables the quickening of the process – the fire of love. When you come to understand that you yourselves are the matter to be cooked and that love is the fire in which you must cook, you will possess the vital knowledge you need to prepare the philosopher's stone and obtain gold.

Nature brings gold and all other metals to maturity by means of heat, so gold is like the food a cook puts in the oven: it requires heat. In nature, gold forms very slowly, as it cooks at a very low temperature. To produce gold in ourselves, we are able to speed up the process by simply turning up the heat. But we must also take care not to burn everything. A trainee alchemist can be compared to a trainee cook who doesn't yet know how to gauge the heat: the meals are either allowed to burn, or else they are undercooked because the heat is so low.

In order to carry through what alchemists call the 'great work' to its successful conclusion and find the philosopher's stone, we must kindle the fire of love within ourselves and learn to control it. It is through love that this process is accelerated: by increasing love we reduce the preparation time. But love also requires great mastery; otherwise, here too, you may well burn everything. Love is the most dreadful fire there is if you are not able to control it, which is why it must always be tempered by wisdom. Now you understand better. The philosopher's stone is that divine state of consciousness that can be attained through love and wisdom.

If fire occupies such a significant position within the alchemical process, it is because life itself is a form of combustion. The maturation of metals, like the ripening of fruit, is nothing other than combustion. Life is sustained by fire, but a fire that doesn't consume, that doesn't char. And, within us, it is the fire of love acting on our psychic matter that brings about maturation. You see how we keep finding these two principles manifesting: the feminine principle – matter – symbolized by water, being worked upon by the masculine principle – spirit – symbolized by fire.[2]

The various containers and implements alchemists use to carry out their work, as well as the tasks themselves, all have their counterpart in the spiritual life. The crucible, the retort, the still and the athanor all represent the human being, who is also the matter on which the operations are carried out. For these operations humans need fire, but a very special kind of fire, one for which great knowledge is required if the right procedures are to be followed.

Well, then, that's clear: we possess the matter, and we also have the container to cook it in, since we are that container. But the fire and the knowledge we must acquire. So the fire is love, but not just any kind of love, not a love that consumes and destroys, no, a love that preserves and gives life. By keeping the fire of love alight, we succeed in extracting the quintessence of our matter, and this quintessence we bring into all our activities, so that everything we do turns to gold.

Alchemists don't tell us what the philosopher's stone is made of. But when it comes to our own matter, we know what this is. Everything in us that is not the pure quintessence of God is matter. I explained this to you when I spoke to you about the different bodies – the physical, astral, mental, causal, buddhic and atmic – that make up a human being. Compared with the divine spark that lives in us, these different bodies are matter, in varying degrees of purity and subtlety, but matter nonetheless.[3] These different kinds of matter are what we must work on, in the knowledge that they correspond to the four elements in the universe.

Each time we bring light and warmth into play, each time we act with wisdom and love, we are forming within ourselves the philosopher's stone, which transmutes all matter into gold; this is how we become true alchemists. Alchemical science is not meant solely for people who will shut themselves away for years in a study, surrounded by indecipherable old treatises and peculiarly-shaped stills. Even if they manage to make gold, of what use will it really be to them? All those years of work will have made them old and worn them out; they won't even be in a fit state to make use of it. They'll soon leave this earth, and when they do they won't be taking the gold with them.

Some will say, 'But you're preaching to the converted! We have no intention of looking for the philosopher's stone to make gold. We're not interested.' That's fine, but inwardly you cannot escape looking for this stone. Sooner or later life will take hold of you and put you in the crucible without asking your opinion.

The life of human beings – their development and evolution – is based on their ability to transform matter, both physical and psychic. Nutrition is the most telling example of this. How can we not marvel at the complexity and subtlety of all the processes set in motion from the moment we put a piece of bread or fruit in our mouth to the moment the quintessence of that food enters our bloodstream to become health, thought, feeling and inspiration?[4]

On the psychic plane, we can also transform everything and make it serve our evolution. And this is still not the whole of the story. Indeed, apart from exceptional cases, the physical body is not able to absorb substances indiscriminately, and not only do we have to choose our food but we also have to prepare it, for there is always something or other that has to be removed – the bones from fish, the rind from cheese, the skin from certain vegetables and fruit, the stones, the pips, etc. But on the psychic plane, everything can be absorbed and transformed, not only the raw energies that exist within us in the form of passions and vices but also the poisons that come from outside us.

True alchemical science is right here in life. Not only does it turn base metals into gold, base metals being everything in our physical and psychic bodies that prevents us receiving light to nourish us and quench our thirst, it also turns pebbles and ordinary stones into precious stones. The form of torture known as stoning, which involves killing men and women by throwing stones at them, is no longer practised in so-called civilized countries. But there are many more ways of throwing stones at a person: suspicion, malicious gossip and slander, for instance. And I have received mountains of those kinds of stones myself. You have no idea of all the accusations that have been, and still are being, levelled at me. Well, instead of allowing myself to be buried beneath those stones, I picked them up one after the other, and I worked on them and turned them into precious stones, and these are what I give you now in the form of light and love.

I won't say I possess the philosopher's stone – you should never use high-flown phrases – but I'm working on it, and every day I accumulate gold, rubies, emeralds, sapphires, topazes and carbuncles to distribute to you. Are you even aware of this? Do you understand I also draw my knowledge from all the stones that have been thrown at me? And, most importantly, are you ready to use the same methods I use, in order to turn everything that's dark and negative within you and outside you into pure gold and precious stones?

You don't have to look for the philosopher's stone anywhere other than in yourself, for there is no philosopher's stone more powerful than the spirit. One day you will attain the state of consciousness in which you experience your spirit, your higher Self, as an immortal, eternal principle, an indestructible entity travelling through space, free to enter everywhere. Then you will understand that nothing is more important than to use this power to work on matter, your own matter, in order to purify it, give it life and revive it.

The philosopher's stone is the quintessence that turns everything into gold, into light, within yourself first of all, but also within all the beings around you because everything extends its influence. This is the sublime dimension of the philosopher's stone.

Notes
1. See *'Cherchez le Royaume de Dieu et sa Justice'*, part VIII, chap. 2, IV: 'L'essence solaire de l'énergie sexuelle'.
2. See *The Splendour of Tiphareth*, CW 10, chap. 21: 'Three kinds of fire'.
3. See *'Et il me montra un fleuve d'eau de la vie'*, part VI: 'Les niveaux de la conscience'.
4. See *The Yoga of Nutrition*, Izvor 204, chap. 1: 'Eating: an act which concerns the whole man'.

Chapter Eleven

THE REGENERATION OF MATTER:
THE CROSS AND THE CRUCIBLE

As we have seen, 3 over 4, as well as the triangle above the square and the pyramid above the cube all symbolize the union of spirit and matter. The cube is a solid with six faces; when developed, it becomes a cross. From the point of view of alchemy, there is much to learn from this change from cube to cross.

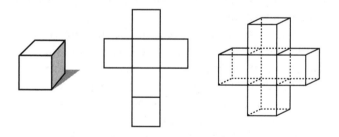

With its compact, condensed shape, the cube is a symbol of stability but also a form denoting boundaries, confinement and imprisonment. And so, as it opens out and develops into a cross, it is as if it were being liberated. If you study this idea more closely, you will come to understand how the cross can become a symbol of liberation. Some of you will be scandalized: 'What? The cross is such an awful means of torture. How can you see it as a symbol of liberation?' My reply would be that you should stop seeing the cross merely as a means of torture, or, as the Christians see it, as the particular means used to torture Jesus.

As a symbol, the cross has its origins in nature itself.[1] Think about it: with the aid of a cross we find our bearings in space – the four cardinal points. The four directions, north-south and east-west, form a cross that gives space its structure. We find this same cross in astrology with the two perpendicular axes, Ascendant-Descendant and Mid-heaven-Nadir, which divide the circle of the zodiac to form the cross of destiny, the cross we must learn to carry if we are to gain immortality.

The vertical line represents the masculine principle and the horizontal line the feminine, the two principles at the origin of all creation in the universe. The masculine principle is associated with fire, which rises, and the feminine principle with water, which spreads outwards. The human being, as a synthesis in miniature of the universe, is also shaped like a cross, with the vertical line from head to feet intersecting the horizontal line of the arms.

And the cross is also a tree, teaching us how to rise from earth to heaven. It is found as the cabbalistic Tree of Life, the sephirotic Tree, where God is shown not only in his different manifestations but also in

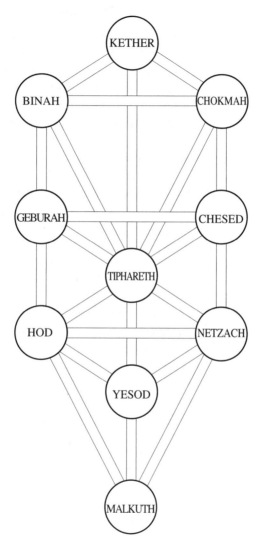

TREE OF LIFE

the angelic hierarchy, in the human being and in the whole cosmos.[2] When I gave you a detailed explanation of the Lord's Prayer, I showed you the relationship between the sephiroth and the various requests which make up the prayer.[3] So the symbol of the cross is also present in the Lord's Prayer.

Also worth mentioning is the ankh, the cross which Egyptian gods and pharaohs hold in their right hand. ♀ This cross can be seen as a key, one which opens the door to the temple of the mysteries. So, as you can see, the cross is one of the richest elements in the language of nature. Every form has something to tell us, and the cross, being an alchemical, cabbalistic, astrological and magical symbol, encapsulates immeasurable knowledge.

The plans of countless churches, cathedrals and basilicas were inspired by the shape of the cross. But how many Christians sense the symbolic dimension of a church when they see one? From the beginning there was the cube, the cube-shaped stone, the very one Jesus referred to when he said to Peter, *'You are Peter, and on this rock I will build my church'*, and the church is the congregation of souls, of the sons and daughters of God. If we can fathom the mysteries of the cross, the doors of eternal life will open for us.

But now let's return to the figure of the cube; when opened out it becomes a two-dimensional cross. Now, if you project it into the third dimension – with height, width and depth – it becomes a solid made up of five cubes *(see diagram, p. 167)*. These five cubes display twenty-two outer surfaces: five on the front, five on the back and twelve around the edges. Now, 22 is the number of letters in the Hebrew alphabet, which stand for the twenty-two elements with which God created the world, as stated in the *Sefer Yetzirah*: 'He engraved and burnished within it twenty-two foundation letters: three mothers and seven doubles and twelve singles.' And 22 is also the number of the Tarot cards in which all of initiatic Science can be found summarized.

As the three-dimensional cross is made up of cubes, it corresponds to the physical plane, the world of realization; the two-dimensional cross corresponds to the spiritual plane; the one-dimensional cross, with its two intersecting straight lines, corresponds to the divine plane, the world of principles. So, the one-dimensional cross sums up and encapsulates the two-dimensional cross, which in turn sums up the three-dimensional cross. But the real cross still remains hidden to us. The real cross is the alchemists' crucible, the container in which they mix, melt and refine the matter of the great work in order to turn it into gold.

Now, why is it so important to move from the cross to the crucible? Because the crucible is where transformation takes place, and where there is transformation there is life. It is a mistake to automatically associate the cross with death, even though this association is made in everyday speech. When the French say they are 'drawing a cross' on something or someone, they are making it known that from then on they consider the thing or person to be written off, non-existent, dead. Christians, with their very narrow understanding of the cross, are the ones responsible for turning it into an object of ridicule. Why choose to see in the cross only suffering, agony and death, when it expresses all of life's potential? Don't the Gospels themselves follow Jesus' death with his resurrection?

Death is not an end; it is not a goal; it is simply a necessary step in preparation for resurrection. Clearly, I am speaking here from a symbolic and spiritual perspective. Resurrection presupposes death; it is a process of transformation that takes place in stages, and from this perspective it can be likened to a birth. This explains why certain alchemists have presented the matter of the great work as a black Madonna, whose task it is to bring the royal Child[4], or the philosopher's stone, into the world.

The matter contained in the crucible is subjected to fire. As it is cooked and cooked again under specific planetary influences, it undergoes a series of changes in colour. First it turns black, which is why it is given the name 'crow's head'. This is the putrefaction stage, also known as 'the work in black'. Next, the matter turns to white, 'the doves of Diana', and finally to red, 'the phoenix', the bird that sacrifices itself in the fire and, three days later, is reborn from its ashes. Black, white and red are the three main colours in alchemical work. But while the matter is in the process of changing from black to red, some alchemists have reported seeing other intermediate colours such as green, yellow and orange, and even sometimes all the colours of the rainbow, which they call 'the peacock's tail'.

Death is never a final state; it is a transition, the passing from an old life to a new one. This is alchemy's main teaching and one that the alchemists drew from their observation of nature. Why, for instance, do they describe the transformation of matter in the great work in terms of a sequence of colours? It is because they observed this sequence in vegetable life. Take fruit trees, for example: with slight variations in shade – since differences abound in nature – they undergo a series of colour changes, always in the same order. During winter, trees are black and bare; in spring, they are white with blossom and green with leaves. Then summer comes: the ripening fruits turn yellow and red, and in autumn the foliage turns red and gold. The process comes to an end with the red and gold; it is the end of the cycle, as it is in alchemical work.

Human beings have to experience the same phases of alchemical work as vegetation does, but within themselves: they die, then they come back to life, but they return with new virtues and powers. Death is never a final ending. Man dies in order to come back to life, or be reborn: in fact, resurrection and rebirth have the same meaning. The black Madonna represents each man or woman who strives to give birth to the divine Child, the higher Self.

And since the alchemists' goal is to take part in nature's work in order to speed up its processes, it makes sense that they would begin by observing these processes, in order to reproduce them in their laboratories. This is why the egg, too, plays an important part in alchemical work. An egg is an organic body through which life is transmitted; it is made up of a shell, albumen and a yolk. The egg, too, embodies the three principles and the four elements. In symbolic terms, fire acted on air to form sulphur (the yolk), air acted on water to form mercury (the albumen), and water acted on earth to form salt (the shell).

And now, why do alchemists call the container in which they place the base matter (or *prima materia*) a 'philosopher's egg'? Because the shell of the egg, with its closed form, can be compared to the crucible, in which the matter is cooked when placed in the alchemical oven (or *athanor*). In the same way, a bird sitting on its egg maintains the required amount of heat for the chick's development. Before the chick comes out of its shell, the putrefaction taking place in the egg can be likened to the putrefaction of the base matter in the crucible. Once the matter turns white, the alchemist may decide to arrest the process and, with what has been achieved so far, will now be able to turn metals into silver. And if the process is seen through to orange-yellow, they can be turned into gold.

White and orange-yellow, the two colours of the egg, are the philosopher's colours. Now it is easy to see how the egg came to be associated with Easter, the festival of resurrection. Some traditions even compare Jesus' resurrection from the tomb to the chick breaking out of its shell.

All these comparisons between natural phenomena, alchemical processes and the life of Jesus shouldn't surprise you. To alchemists, the analogies are very clear: in the sacrifice of Jesus on the cross for the salvation of the world, they see the death of the base matter, from which they make the philosopher's stone, which transmutes metals into gold. Jesus' body on the cross represents that matter which must die before it can come back to life. It is the same process of transmutation at work. And this also explains the interpretation that alchemists give to the spear thrust into Jesus' side by the Roman soldier. The Gospels tell us that, to make sure Jesus was dead, a Roman soldier pierced his side with a spear. Now, in alchemical symbolism, the spear represents the masculine principle, the spirit, which is working on the feminine principle, matter.

In some alchemical treatises the same concept is present in the image of a dragon run through by a spear, for the dragon also represents matter, the feminine principle, since it is linked to the world of water.[5] You will find the spear also in the hands of the archangel Michael and St. George, both of whom, according to tradition, confronted and defeated a dragon.

Many countries have folktales that recount adventures with the same meaning. But in those, it is a knight who has to kill a dragon, in order to reach a princess kept prisoner in a castle where treasure is piled high. The knight is the alchemist working on the *prima materia,* the primordial chaos, or the dragon whose open jaws spew foul emanations. The knight must kill the dragon with a red-hot spear. In the same way, at a certain stage of the process, the alchemist has to defeat a substance that produces poisonous fumes. In the crucible – on the cross, in other words – they run it through with their spear; the substance dies and returns to life. Matter and the spear always have work to do together.

Alchemists refer to the base matter by various names: mercury, the dragon, the humid, the radical, the universal solvent. And the spear also has synonyms: sulphur, the magnet, steel. The alchemist Basile Valentin calls the spear 'lion' and the matter 'eagle'. The eagle attacks the lion, and they engage in a terrible battle. This battle has also been described as a confrontation between two dogs. In this confrontation, which again represents spirit striving to control matter, matter is defeated and dies but then comes back to life and gives birth to the philosopher's stone, the Child-King, the Christ who has the power to heal lepers. And what are these lepers? The base metals, meaning the defects and vices, of which human beings can only be cured if they appeal to the power of the Christ within.

The Gospels, therefore, can also be understood and interpreted in the light of alchemical science. On the face of it, they are simply giving an account of the life of one man, Jesus, born two thousand years ago in Palestine, but while they recount the different stages of his life, from birth to death and resurrection, they are in fact also describing alchemical processes. Alchemy was condemned by the Church, when the popes themselves practised it. And if you study the sculptures both on the outside and the inside of cathedrals such as the Notre-Dame in Paris or the Notre-Dame in Chartres, you will discover what knowledge Christians possessed at the time such monuments were built.

The builders of these cathedrals possessed alchemical knowledge, as architecture and sculpture amply testify. Thus, they carved in stone all the stages through which matter passes during the preparation of the philosopher's stone. Even the Old Testament story of the Flood as shown in these buildings can be viewed from an alchemical perspective. Rain falls for forty days and forty nights; now, 40 is the number for death. The ark, in which Noah and his family shut themselves away, together with a pair from every species of animal, represents the alchemist's vessel in which the transmutation occurs. As for Horev, the crow, and Iona, the dove, which Noah releases one after the other to see whether terra firma has reappeared,[6] these represent two essential stages of the great work: the transition from black to white.

And since the creation of gold is the outcome of a long and difficult undertaking, some researchers have also claimed they have found descriptions of alchemical work in ancient legends, such as those from Greek mythology. The most famous among these legends are those about Jason and his companions sailing with the Argo to capture the Golden Fleece, or, of course, Hercules gathering the golden apples in the garden of the Hesperides.

What makes alchemists' accounts so difficult to understand is the fact that, because they wish both to reveal and hide their knowledge, they never name anything clearly and openly but use figures, images and symbols, to which they give meanings known only to themselves. But they do not use them in a random way, and the meanings are not arbitrary. Thus, colours, illustrations drawn from the animal, vegetable and mineral worlds, geometrical figures, mythological characters and episodes from the life of Jesus can easily be interpreted by those who have studied closely the origin and nature of symbolic language.

Where do symbols come from? They originate in the relationship between the universal Soul and the human unconscious. The connections perceived by the unconscious have been given concrete expression in objects, figures from the mineral, vegetable or animal world or geometric forms. So symbols are explained by the fact that the same laws govern both creation and its creatures and that we therefore instinctively perceive the connections between the different worlds. However, it must also be understood that, since symbolic language is the expression of our life at its deepest level, when we come across symbols in initiatic Science or in particular works of art, we need to experience them if we are to understand them.

If you do not experience what a symbol represents, you will never understand it, even if you are given the interpretation. So you must go deep, deep inside yourself and experience the symbols in order to know what they mean. This rule is particularly true in the case of the symbol of the cross.

So those were a few words about the cross, but the cross of life, not the cross of death. When you understand the living cross, everything begins to speak to you – not only nature but myths and legends and all the sacred texts. Although the symbols through which the knowledge is revealed differ from one culture to another, or from one period to another, that knowledge is always one and the same but in many different guises.

For centuries, Christians have focused on the cross; they contemplate it, they wear it on their body, and they think they know it. But no, they don't yet know it. What proof is there of this? It is plain to see that the base metals inside them, namely their weaknesses and vices, have not dissolved, and the reason for this is that they haven't known how to light the divine fire of love within, in their own crucible. What kind of love is this that is unable to dissolve metals?... Love is the power that makes a rose bloom at the centre of the cross, for the true cross is a symbol of resurrection and eternal life.

Notes

1. See *'Cherchez le Royaume de Dieu et sa Justice'*, part VI, chap. 2, IV: 'La croix'.
2. See *Angels and Other Mysteries of The Tree of Life*, Izvor 236.
3. See *'Cherchez le Royaume de Dieu et sa Justice'*, part I: 'La prière dominicale', pp. 34-36.
4. See *Sons and Daughters of God*, Izvor 240, chap. IX: 'The Birth of the Christ-Child'.
5. See *The Book of Revelations: a Commentary*, Izvor 230, chap. 11: 'The Archangel Mikhaël casts out the dragon'; chap. 12: 'The dragon spews water at the woman'; chap. 13: 'The beast from the sea and the beast from the land'.
6. See *Cosmic Balance*, Izvor 237, chap. 10: 'Iona, principle of life – Horev, principle of death'.

Chapter Twelve

THE MAY DEW

In their wish to influence matter, some alchemists were ambitious not just to transform it but to bring it to life. The creation of the homunculus[1], for example, which I have already told you about, was an alchemical venture, as was the process called *palingenesis*.

Palingenesis (from the Greek *palin* 'again' and *genesis* 'birth') is a phenomenon whereby alchemists claimed to be able to bring withered plants back to life, having first reduced them to ashes. They would place the ashes in a flask, add a small amount of a liquid called *spiritus universalis* 'universal spirit' and hermetically seal it. This liquid was prepared from May dew which had been exposed to heavenly influences for forty days and forty nights, giving it, they said, the property of fixing universal spirit. Having combined this liquid with the ashes, they would heat the mixture and, soon after, would see the plant appear in its etheric form. The plant would remain as long as the heat was maintained; then the form would gradually vanish. The experiment could be repeated at will.

Although it is interesting to know of these experiments, it is much more important to understand how we can use the powers of life to undertake regenerative work on ourselves. From the moment we decide to rely on the spirit alone, on the divine entity that lives within us, we set a whole process in motion: elements or forces arrive from space to work on us, attracted as by a magnet. This process of regeneration is possible for each one of us, but only on condition that we first work on matter, our own matter.

Alchemists also say that when the matter they are working on is finally ready, the universal spirit enters it and infuses it with its powers, so that only a very small amount of this matter is needed to turn metals into gold. And with us it is the same: the spirit doesn't descend just anywhere; it is up to us to prepare our own matter to receive it. This is a very lengthy process, but when we are ready the spirit comes down, and then our thoughts, feelings and actions are marked by its seal.

Let's add a few more words about this *spiritus universalis* that alchemists prepare with the May dew. But first of all, what is this dew? It is condensed water vapour, which settles at night as fine droplets, under the effect of the earth's radiation. Water makes a tremendous journey from earth to sky and back again.[2] As it evaporates into the atmosphere it is being purified, the different layers through which it passes each acting like a filter ridding it of impurities.

Now, it is said in alchemical treatises that, one night, when the water is finally ready, it is visited by the universal spirit, which fertilizes it, impregnating it with its quintessences. When it falls again as dew on grass, on flowers and on all vegetation, it is happy because it knows it is bringing life.

The effects of dew are more powerful than those of ordinary water. Dew feeds and waters plants, even in barren regions where not a single drop of rain falls for months on end. Without dew, all vegetation would die. When we think of dew, we usually have in mind the last part of its journey, when it comes down and settles on the earth. But we shouldn't forget that before water can become dew it has first to form a vapour that rises up into the atmosphere, where it is fertilized by the universal spirit as it passes through. Because it has first risen, when it condenses again on its way back down to earth it brings with it all the life-giving elements that make up the salt of the spirit.

You may say, 'But why do alchemists use the May dew especially?' Because the month of May, coming as it does approximately halfway through spring, corresponds to the period when nature is at the peak of its renewal. The first three weeks of May are under the influence of Taurus, the sign of fertility, where Venus, the planet of generation, is in domicile, and where the moon, the symbol of the feminine principle, is exalted. It is therefore a time when nature receives fresh currents of energy circulating throughout space, and the water vapour is impregnated with these currents before falling again as dew.

Within every man and woman there is a substance, symbolized by water and known as the soul, which is capable of rising to the highest regions of the spiritual world. When it does, the universal spirit, as it passes through, lightly touches the soul with its breath, and the alchemical operation of transmutation can begin, whereby base metals are transmuted into gold. Clearly, when water rises up in the atmosphere, it doesn't do so of its own accord. It is the sun that draws it up by transforming it into vapour. As for us, we are both matter and spirit, and thanks to the power of the spirit – our own sun – we are able to make our own water – our psychic matter – rise. But do not misunderstand me: while I often make use of analogies to shed light on certain inner life processes, I am not so naïve as to believe that physical processes are precisely equivalent to spiritual ones.

Although I began reading books on alchemy at a very early age, I was immediately struck by the correspondences I found between the transmutation of physical matter described there and the work spiritual people must accomplish on their psychic matter in order to transform it. These are the very correspondences I am always mentioning to you. In order to prepare the philosopher's stone, alchemists seek to capture and condense a quintessence from the sun. This quintessence increases the vibratory rate of metals when it comes into contact with them and thus achieves their transmutation. We, too, possess the quintessence of solar origin that alchemists attempt to condense: it is the divine principle, which we must strive to reach each day, very high in ourselves, and draw down through our different bodies into the physical body.

We call this divine principle within us the higher Self.[3] It is our true Self, and this true Self is always higher than we ourselves are. To use another image, I would say that we must attempt to throw ropes up to it, as mountaineers do when they haul themselves up by hitching their rope to higher and higher pitons fastened to the rock. We can only find our true Self by projecting ourselves again and again towards the heights. This is why the image of the sun, the symbol of the spirit, can have such a beneficial effect on our inner life.

You can also read in some treatises that the best time period for beginning alchemical work is when the sun has entered Aries and the moon is in Taurus. On the wheel of the zodiac, Taurus follows Aries.[4] Then comes Gemini, Mercury's domicile; now, to alchemists, Mercury is a symbol for the philosopher's stone, the child of the Sun and the Moon. You may recall that in mythology Mercury (or Hermes) is always represented as a child or youth, who is active, intelligent, ingenious and clever with his hands and, therefore, capable of working on matter to transform it. So, even in the zodiac, the foundations of alchemical work are to be found.

They are also present in the sephirotic Tree. When we studied the symbols attached to the sephiroth on the central pillar, we saw that the philosopher's stone is associated with Malkuth, the Earth, that is to say with concretization, materialization.[5] Above is Yesod, the Moon, the feminine principle, and above this Tiphareth, the Sun, the masculine principle. The sequence Sun, Moon, Earth reproduces the sequence Aries, Taurus, Gemini, in which realization is the fruit of the union between the masculine and the feminine principles.

When alchemists say the work should begin at the time when the Sun enters Aries and the Moon Taurus, they mean that, for creation to take place, spirit and matter must meet at the time most propitious for their manifestation. The Sun, the masculine principle, is represented in us by the spirit and the mind; the Moon, the feminine principle, by the soul and the heart. So the feminine principle in us – the Moon, or water, symbolizing matter – must constantly seek to rise, to reach upwards to the fire of the Sun, the fire of the spirit, in order to be fertilized and then fall again as life-giving dew.

In your everyday life, depending on circumstances, you may pass through different inner states, some quite ordinary, even gross at times, and others poetic, luminous and spiritual. So from now on, if you come to experience a moment of true elevation, consider it as a peak you have reached through your efforts, and endeavour to remain there. Let this state act as an inner tuning-fork, sounding the note for all the other forces that dwell within you, so that you create inner unity and harmony.

Notes

1. See '*Et il me montra un fleuve d'eau de la vie',* part I: 'Mystère de la vie, mystère de Dieu', p. 13.
2. See *The Mysteries of Fire and Water,* Izvor 232, chaps. 11 and 12: 'The cycle of water'.
3. See '*Et il me montra un fleuve d'eau de la vie',* part VI, chap. 3: 'Le Moi supérieur. La descente du Saint-Esprit'.
4. See *Love and Sexuality* (part 1), CW 14, chap. III: 'Taking the bull by the horns – the caduceus of Mercury'.
5. See *Angels and Other Mysteries of The Tree of Life,* Izvor 236, chap. 5: 'The sephiroth of the central pillar'.

Chapter Thirteen

THE GROWTH OF THE DIVINE SEED

Alchemical work is about regeneration, and this work is mentioned in different forms by every religion. The Christian religion presents it as the transformation of the old Adam into the Christ. The old Adam is represented by lead, Saturn, while the Christ is the new man, who has succeeded in acquiring the precious qualities of gold, the Sun. And what are these qualities? Not only does gold shine with a wonderful brilliance, it is also immutable and will not corrode. Of course, we can never completely achieve this ideal in our physical body – and anyway that's not so important – but in our spiritual body, our body of glory, we can.[1]

This spiritual body is present in seed form in even the most sinful of humans; the Creator himself gave it to them as a seed, a germ, that he placed in them as the sign, the mark, the imprint, of their divine origin. If they work on this seed, they too will rediscover the divine model according to which they were created; they too will then be able to rebuild the kingdom of God within. And for this seed to be able to grow, it must be exposed each day to the sun of wisdom and love.

If we can be regenerated and brought back to life, it is because we already possess at least one atom as the starting point for this rebuilding. Alchemists say that, in order to make gold, they must have at least one atom of gold at the outset as a seed. In nature, nothing can reproduce without a seed: not plants, nor animals, nor men. And this same law also applies to alchemical operations: alchemists need at least one particle of gold. Through the power of the philosopher's stone, this one particle is able to turn any amount of molten metal into gold.

The alchemical process is therefore similar to the growth or the multiplication of a seed. A grain of wheat at first yields one ear and then, one day, a whole wheatfield! Similarly, a speck of gold can 'multiply' to infinity for anyone who knows the secret. We too possess this speck of gold, this divine seed from the Creator. Now he has given it to us, nothing and no one has the power to take it away from us or make us lose it, but it is up to us to become aware of this seed and to awaken it, to give it life so that it develops into a tree…[2] a temple…[3] the New Jerusalem…[4] the Christ-Child…[5] So many images and symbols have been used to convey this reality!

All human beings possess this seed, but they can spend their whole life without doing anything with it, because they have never even heard that it exists. Some might have a vague idea or feeling about it, but they don't know where or how to look for it, much less how to work with it. Once they do know, the words 'life' and 'resurrection' will take on real meaning for them.[6]

Life feeds on life. A woman who has received a seed of life into her womb feeds it for nine months with her own life. When the seed has been fed in this way, it grows to give birth to a child, endowed with limbs and organs that allow it in turn to be able to eat, breathe, touch, smell, see, hear, move, think and work. The same applies to the divine seed within us, if we know how to make it grow, for we have the same possibilities on the spiritual level as on the physical. And any work we do on the spiritual level will in time bring about changes on the physical too.

So we don't need to ask ourselves whether we are capable of carrying out the same operations on metals as the alchemists describe in their treatises. All we need to know is that they can be achieved within us, on the spiritual level, and how to go about it. I shall give you a method, and even if it were the only one I had ever given you – which is obviously not the case! – you would have all you need for your transformation. So here is the method. If you have discovered a truth, a divine idea, think of it as a seed you can place in the soil. Once you have sown it in your soil, that is to say, in your heart or soul, watch it grow: you will experience how life is born and how it develops in yourself and in the whole universe.

Why is it that religion has become a meaningless practice for many believers (not to mention non-believers, which is a whole other matter!)? It is because they don't know how to work with the truths it contains. And there is only one way to work with these truths. They must be sown, just as seeds are sown, yes, sown in your inner soil, and every day they should be tended, watered and kept warm. The weeds that grow all around them and threaten to suffocate them should be removed, and you must also get rid of the bugs about to nibble at them. What does this mean? It means that, if we want the truths we have sown in our spiritual soil to grow within us, we must feed them and we must prevent lower thoughts and feelings from coming to attack them like parasites.

I myself have sown many seeds that Jesus left us in the Gospels, and I water them and watch over them, and so they grow. Religious truths cannot really be understood by the mind alone. They must be sown and planted within, until they become flesh and bone. And this is what we are doing here, when we go to contemplate the sunrise in the morning, allowing its light, warmth and life to pervade us. We are helping the seeds to germinate, to grow, to blossom and give fruit.

The seed planted in the ground contains the potential tree. No one can make out the roots, stem, leaves, flowers or fruits, and yet they will soon emerge into the light of day. For a tree to come from this seed, four conditions are necessary: it must be put in the earth, watered, allowed to breathe and be provided with warmth and sunlight. All four elements are therefore present: earth, water, air and fire.[7] As the roots sink into the soil, a small stem appears, which becomes a trunk, and the trunk divides into branches, which grow buds. When the buds burst open, leaves and flowers appear, and the flowers become fruit. Eventually, the fruit produces seeds again, and the cycle begins anew.

The tree can also be seen as a symbol of alchemical work. The roots correspond to mercury, the feminine principle, the mother, the primordial water; the branches, which become covered in leaves, allowing sunlight to produce photosynthesis, correspond to sulphur, the masculine principle, the father, the creative fire; finally, the trunk and everything in the tree that will grow to become hard, compact matter correspond to salt, the child. When we study the tree from the perspective of alchemical science, we see its true, cosmic dimension.

Everything that exists in the universe passes through the same stages, and these successive stages are what we call life. Depending on the beings involved and the different kingdoms or planes where they appear, some processes are longer, others shorter. What is remarkable about trees, and fruit trees in particular, is that these processes are repeated every year without fail, with the four seasons as their four stages. To stress the importance of these stages, the initiatic tradition has placed each of them under the influence of an archangel.

The seed is under the influence of the archangel Gabriel, who condenses and solidifies the elements. It is placed in the earth at the darkest and coldest time of the year, and Gabriel transmits memory to it through hereditary genes, which maintain its characteristics from one generation to the next. He introduces all the distinctive features and properties of the plant into the seed, condensing them into the tiny mass that will hold the plant's future in latent form. And he does the same with the semen of animals and of human beings. Each generation preserves all its own characteristics in its chromosomes – the memory is never lost.

In contrast to the archangel Gabriel, who concentrates energies, the archangel Raphael frees them. To do this, he first makes the seed die, so that everything it contains can manifest as roots, a stem, branches, leaves, flowers and fruit, which will give new seeds. So far, the seed has been a frozen, paralysed being, stagnating for maybe thousands of years, waiting for the right conditions. The seed appears to be dead, rather like a body left in a coffin. But in spring, with the return of warmth, wherever there are seeds a resurrection takes place: every seed is like a small grave half-opening. The archangel Raphael sets to work, the stone is removed by the angels of the hierarchy of the *Bnei Elohim,* which he commands, and the seed sends out a shoot.[8]

The cause of this resurrection is warmth, which must further increase for maturation to take place. The archangel Uriel is responsible for this: Uriel is fire, flames, the high heat of summer. It's a long time now since the tree flowered. But what is a flower? It's the organ of a plant that's closest to the animal kingdom. This animal part of the plant possesses sensitivity, something akin to a nervous system: it opens in the light and closes in the dark. We could even go so far as to say that the plant's astral body is formed in the flower. In fact, the flower is the sexual organ of the plant, where fertilization takes place. And so Uriel works with heat so that the flowers will produce fruit.

In autumn the archangel Michael comes to separate the fruit from the tree, just as he also separates the good grain from the tares. During the summer, the good and the bad, the useful and the harmful have grown together, and they need to be separated and sorted. This is Michael's role: he cuts through the ties with his sword. But this separation must take place at the right moment, just as with the birth of a child. The child is like a fruit that detaches from its mother, the tree, but this separation must happen at a precise point in time; the umbilical cord must not be cut prematurely. The archangel Michael comes to separate mother and child at the right moment.

So when autumn comes, the archangel Michael, at the head of the hierarchy of the *Malakhim* 'the virtues', separates the fruit from the tree, and the casing and seed from the fruit. Animals or human beings are often instrumental in removing the skin and pips or stone from fruit, before eating its flesh. By doing this, they help nature realize its full potential for renewal, so that species are able to survive. Without this separation, there would be no new life.

In autumn too, the chaff is separated from the good grain, to be put away in the loft. In the same way, the archangel Michael pulls the human soul from the body, which is its casing. And, in a way, the soul is also placed in the loft, that is to say, in a peaceful place in the invisible world where there are neither mice nor diseases, and where the master of the house watches over it. Later, it will be sown again, in other words, sent to earth to reincarnate. Once more it will be winter for the soul; it will suffer, remembering the place it has left and yearning for the peace and light that reigned there, and it will complain, 'I was cared for and protected there; now I've been hurled into a dark place where they forget about me. Often they don't even know I exist.' Where is this? In the mother's womb, for a new life has begun, and it's true that it does sometimes take a while for a woman to know she is carrying this life inside her.

You see now how we can read the cycles of our own life in the life of the tree.

If we stay with the image of the tree, there are many more things we can discover. The tree is present in the Bible from the beginning of the book of *Genesis*[9] right through to the end of the book of *Revelations*.[10] So, learn how to look at trees, to enter deeply into their being. You will feel, and perhaps one day even see, the entities that live in them and take care of them. Even if you don't see them, they will teach you year after year about the science of seeds. They will teach you how to develop this speck of gold that was given to you by the Creator from his own quintessence so that you would be able to transmute matter, not only in your soul but in your body as well.

Notes

1. See *'You are Gods'*, part IX, chap. 4: 'The body of glory' and *'Il me montra un fleuve d'eau de la vie'*, part IV, chap. 4: 'L'édification du corps glorieux'.

2. See *'You are Gods'*, part III, chap. 3: 'From seed to tree'.

3. See *Creation: Artistic and Spiritual,* Izvor 223, chap. 11: 'A living masterpiece' and chap. 12: 'Building the temple'.

4. See *'Cherchez le Royaume de Dieu et sa Justice'*, part VIII, chap. 4: 'Et il me montra la ville sainte, Jérusalem, qui descendait du ciel'.

5. See *Sons and Daughters of God,* Izvor 240, chap. 9: 'The Birth of the Christ-Child'.

6. See *La Fête de Pâques, 'Je suis la résurrection et la vie'*, brochure 308.

7. See *'Et il me montra un fleuve d'eau de la vie'*, part XI, chap. 2: 'Les racines de la matière, les quatre Animaux saints', and chap. 3: 'Les quatre éléments dans la construction de nos différents corps'.

8. See *Langage symbolique, langage de la nature,* OC 8, chap. VII: 'Le premier jour du printemps'.

9. See *'You are Gods'*, pp. 32-34 and pp. 435-436.

10. See *'Et il me montra un fleuve d'eau de la vie'*, part XII, chap. 3: 'Et sur les deux bords du fleuve il y avait un arbre de vie'.

Chapter Fourteen

THE GOLD OF TRUE KNOWLEDGE:
THE ALCHEMIST AND
THE GOLD PROSPECTOR

Even those who know nothing about alchemy and have no interest in the practice know it has something to do with making gold. This is obviously far from enough, but that's how it is. Gold has always caught people's imagination. Why? Because it puts them in touch with the sun, the source of life. Gold comes from the sun and is condensed sunlight; this is what gives it such real value. The sun produces etheric gold, which the earth then fixes; for billions of years the sun's rays have travelled through space and penetrated to the very depths of the earth, where entities work to change them into matter. And now we can collect gold from the earth, just as in summer we pick ripe fruit from a tree.[1]

Human beings fight each other for gold, kill each other for gold, but this is not what the sun wants. What it wants is for something good and magnificent to be realized in humans through the agency of gold. They have seen the sun shine above their heads for long enough, and by now they should have understood its plans and learned to use gold's abundant beneficial forces, not only for their physical health but also for the development of their spiritual bodies. For it is possible to reverse the process of the condensation of gold and recover the light, warmth and power of the sun.

Gold will never lose its value as long as the sun exists, since the 'bank' issuing it is in the sun. Ambassadors owe their power to the nation that sent them; they are received with respect and consideration, because the entire country they represent stands behind them. Behind gold is the sun; this is why it is admired and sought after. If the sight of gold can bring about such a state of well-being and joy, of expansion in the solar plexus, it is because gold possesses the life and radiance of the sun.

Lead is used to screen certain harmful vibrations, but gold offers much stronger protection than lead, and it could also be used to make screens that would receive, and even amplify, solely beneficial influences. Yes, imagine a tiny cell, lined with gold leaf, where you could go to be with yourself, to do spiritual work for the benefit of yourself and the whole world. It would be worth trying such an experiment, but since the cost of setting it up would be too expensive, at least for the time being, it's obviously out of the question!

In the meantime, we must at least be aware of the gold we already possess, so that we can work with it. For gold is also present in our physical body. Yes, there is gold in our blood, and this gold gives us the energy to work and thus acquire wealth. And it also protects us against illness, as it emits a type of vibration that bars the way to germs and viruses. And, finally, it is gold in a different form that illumines our consciousness; those who possess it can acquire wisdom and penetrate the secrets of nature. No doubt it's useful to amass gold in one's coffers, but it's so much more useful, essential even, to increase the gold in oneself!

Alchemists, then, have sought the philosopher's stone because of its ability to change metals into gold, to heal illness, to prolong life and, lastly, to reveal the secrets of nature. So, there are three types of gold: material wealth, health and wisdom. Yes, wisdom, which shouldn't be confused with the theoretical knowledge acquired from books, for that kind of knowledge won't teach you to find your way along life's paths.

Book knowledge is good only for a time, and it is limited in its application and effectiveness. When troubles arise, from the outside world or from within yourself, that knowledge leaves you without help; you feel weak, disorientated and powerless. You search your inner coffers, but what do you find? Worthless notes the sun's banks will give you nothing for. The sun spirits will say, 'We don't recognize those notes here!' And even if you can prove this is the currency on earth, they'll reply, 'Maybe, but it's not the currency here. The only tender here is true gold.'

Gold represents true knowledge, knowledge that is, above all, light; initiatic knowledge, which enables us to read the book of nature, to develop ourselves, so that we can enter the service of the

Lord. And why would we enter the service of the Lord? Because that is where we can find freedom.[2] Yes, this is the way true gold teaches us, and not only does it teach us but it shows us how best to use our time. What discoveries, then, and what journeys there are in store for those who possess this gold! Now you know which gold I mean and how to obtain it through your spiritual work. All human knowledge is worthless when compared to a few grams of true gold, for it is only with this gold that you will obtain security, support and protection.

Disciples of an initiatic school are like alchemists, looking for the philosopher's stone that will instantly turn all metals into gold. And at the same time they are like prospectors for gold, engaged in sifting sand from a riverbed. Working on the philosopher's stone is such a lengthy and difficult undertaking that, even if alchemists devote their life to it, they cannot be certain of attaining their goal. But, for disciples, this is no reason to become discouraged: even if they don't find the secret of instantly transforming all their matter into gold, into light, none of their efforts are ever wasted. In fact, just like the prospector for gold who finds at least one nugget each day, the disciple also gains a nugget, a drop of light, each day, and in this way, one nugget at a time, one drop at a time, draws closer to perfection.

So, the conclusion we can draw is simple: we should never stop working and making efforts, but we should constantly exercise our will. Yes, so often it's the will that is lacking! Humans hope for the good, they desire it and aspire to it, but there it ends; they go no further. They don't make use of their will to achieve the good outcome they desire. They continue to live as they have always done, instinctively, mechanically and carelessly. Of course, daily life requires a modicum of willpower; you have to get out of bed in the morning, go to work, take care of your family, and so on, but everyone does that; there's no great merit in that.

The will I am talking about is a decision of the heart and the mind, inspired by the soul and the spirit. Do you wish to develop your will? Begin by studying yourself in order to know yourself, and then resolve to direct your inner life in such a way that you have no alternative but to develop your qualities and correct your faults.

It's true there are people who show an extraordinary amount of will to succeed in society, to eliminate competitors or opponents. In such situations, it would be better, of course, if they were less determined, for they are only putting their will at the service of their lower nature, whereas the Creator gave us a will to use for the opposite, as an instrument for our higher nature so that we place it in the service of a high ideal. How are we to do this? First, with light, with the understanding of essential truths. As soon as you have understood an essential truth, you must use your will to put it into practice, in the knowledge that this is the only way to truly understand it.

Stating truths is easy; anyone can go and find them in the works of a few sages and then repeat them parrot-fashion. By doing this, they may even earn the respect of those who are too blind to see how weak and broken they are inside. But deceiving the blind is no great achievement! In any case, there are others who are not deceived: the beings of light in the invisible world. And it is these entities, in fact, whose respect we must earn, and we can earn it by putting into practice the truths revealed to us by initiates. These truths are weapons, and we will never find better ones to win life's battles with, but if we have no arms to use them, that is, the will to apply them, they will remain ineffective.

It is said that during the reign of the Ottoman sultan Mehmet II, known as the Conqueror, a warrior had become famous for winning twenty-two victories over enemy armies. This was at the time when they fought with sabres! Well, one day, the sultan asked to be brought the sabre that was always winning battles and must, as he believed, possess exceptional properties. So it was brought to him. He took hold of it and turned it this way and that, but the sabre was quite ordinary, and the sultan, disappointed, sent it back, saying he was not interested in such a mediocre weapon. When the hero who had emerged victorious from so many battles heard of the sultan's reaction, he exclaimed, 'But he only saw the sabre; he didn't see my arm. It was my arm that won the victories.'

I too give you a sabre, that is, methods which are effective but only if you apply them. Even a very small knife can work wonders if you practise handling it every day, and a single match can set fire to a whole town. You can also do tremendous work using a seemingly insignificant method; it's all in the arm, that is, the will. Resolve, therefore, to use the knowledge and methods you have received, and one day you will win the twenty-two battles of initiation: three for the physical, the spiritual and the divine worlds, seven for the planets and twelve for the constellations of the zodiac. Interpret that as you may…

In the language of symbols, the will, the fighting force that triumphs over enemies and disperses inner and outer darkness, is represented by the sabre, the sword or the two-edged sword. But these weapons don't just have a symbolic function; they can be used. Initiatic Science explains that evil spirits assail human beings by enveloping them in a thick fluid, like a black cloud, but if a sword is pointed at this fluid it disintegrates, and the dark entities take flight.

It is said that Paracelsus owned a sword which he used to repel the waves of hate that followed him everywhere. His knowledge and personality had made him many enemies, who plotted his downfall. So when he felt attacked in the invisible by the dark forces they projected onto him, he would wield his sword, brandishing it in all directions. But obviously it's not enough to wave a weapon around if you wish to rid yourself of dark entities; you must already possess this weapon inside yourself: namely, a trained will, directed by lucid, powerful thought and sustained by the feeling of disinterested love. Yes, physical weapons are not much help in spiritual life, and I don't advise you to use them. To win true victories, simply work with your mind, your heart and your will.[3]

Every day some new aspects of truth are revealed to you, and every day you receive a few particles of light, a few rays from the divine sun. Can you sense them? What are you still waiting for? All you lack is the willingness to make an effort, to be patient and tenacious. You'll say, 'But it takes such a long, long time; the years go by…' Yes, for us it is a long time, but for the universal Spirit that lives in eternity it isn't long. You too must learn to live in eternity, and then you will have a different perception of time.

The patience and tenacity shown by the alchemists – those are the qualities you must try hard to acquire! Some of their stories are well known. They would keep working for years and sometimes find nothing, or very little! But they never became discouraged, so convinced were they there was something to be found, something more precious than the treasures of any palace, something worth every sacrifice.

Alchemists (chemists as well, for that matter) who do not work correctly fail in their experiments: either they don't mix the elements in the right proportions or they mix what shouldn't be mixed, the result of which can be an explosion. It's the same with people on a spiritual path: if they don't obtain a result, it isn't because the teaching they received is wrong or the methods they have been given are ineffective; it's that they haven't gone about things in the right way. And, mostly, they are in a hurry, because they are lazy. They soon tire of having to make an effort, and they think there are quick ways to get round difficulties.

Of course, it's a bit like that with medicine: you take some tablets, have a few injections, and you might be back on your feet. Unfortunately, with spiritual work it never happens like that. There are no tablets and no injections available, and you have to work for a long time on your own matter, cooking it, kneading it and shaping it. And anyone claiming to reveal secrets that will change you and your whole life from one day to the next is a charlatan. What *can* happen suddenly is that a truth is revealed, or you are shown a new direction to take, but after that you have to work and work…

Even if you are offered all the treasures in the world, in order to truly appreciate them you will still have to learn to do something with them; otherwise, you will remain as poor inside as if you had nothing. Imagine you're seated at a table that's covered with the most delicious dishes. Even then you still have to make the effort to reach out with your hand to bring the food to your mouth and then make the effort to chew it. Yet again, the example of nutrition is very instructive! Whatever you are given, it is always up to you to make the physical, emotional or mental effort needed to really make it your own. Until you understand this, there is no point speaking of spirituality.

So many of you imagine it would be enough to find an extraordinary method that gives results in a short time! In fact, it's exactly the opposite: you need only simple methods and a lot of time. You have to behave like an alchemist and like a prospector for gold. In order to find light, peace, love and strength, make a particular gesture or take a few deep breaths, or concentrate on saying a formula or a prayer, and gradually you will feel yourself back in rhythm with cosmic harmony. When this happens, Nature will say to you, 'I recognize these words and movements. Their vibration is in harmony with all that is most beautiful and luminous in me. Here you are, I give you my blessings.' Yes, it's very simple, but you have to do it again every day, and several times a day, all through your life.[4]

Contrary to what some people believe, alchemy is not a branch of chemistry. Qualified chemists with a well-equipped laboratory at their disposal can successfully perform any experiment. But it's not the same for alchemists. It isn't enough for them to bring together all the material requirements for their work; they must also prepare their soul, their mind, their heart and even their physical body, which they endeavour to keep in a state of true purity. Even if they haven't yet succeeded in conquering all their weaknesses, nature can grant them success. But, if their successes aren't to turn into traps, they must make sure they make good use of them. It is possible to acquire power over matter, but such power is dangerous for those whose priority is not to work on themselves, as this alone will keep them out of temptation's way.

The alchemists have a motto: *ora et labora* 'pray and work'. Yes, pray first, and then work.[5] Why? To give the best direction to their work, for although work can make human beings greater and nobler, all the tasks and goals they set themselves in their work are not of equal value. You need to know for whom you are working and to what end. And only prayer can bring us light and direct us in what we do, since it connects us to the divine world. Thanks to prayer, light is brought to bear on how we can use our energies for the good of all. Some people claim that work is prayer. Yes, in a way, that's true. Nevertheless, it is better to pray before we work.

One day, you will understand that you receive true gold here, gold that will be of use to you even beyond this earthly life. So ask for nothing else. Pray and work!

Notes
1. See *'Cherchez le Royaume de Dieu et sa Justice'*, part IV, chap. 6: 'À l'origine de l'or, la lumière'.
2. See *Freedom, the Spirit Triumphant,* Izvor 211, chap. 6: 'True freedom: a consecration of self'.
3. See *'Et il me montra un fleuve d'eau de la vie'*, part V, chap. 3: 'Le pilier de la Rigueur', pp. 162-163; part VII, chap. 5: 'Je

suis le chemin, la vérité et la vie', pp. 286-287, and part IX, chap. 3: 'Le savoir de l'unité', pp. 366-368.

4. See *The Faith That Moves Mountains,* Izvor 238, chap. 13: 'Rabota, Vreme, Vera: work, time, faith'.

5. See *'Cherchez le Royaume de Dieu et sa Justice',* part III, chap. 3: 'La prière'.

BIBLICAL REFERENCES

Chapter 1

'The letter kills, but the Spirit gives life' – *2 Corinthians 3:6, p. 13.*

Sacerdotal prayer – *John 17, p. 15.*

'Now I am going to him who sent me…' – *John 16:5-12, p. 16.*

'I, John… was in the spirit' – *Revelations 1:9, p. 18.*

'I know a person in Christ' – *2 Corinthians 12:2, p. 18.*

Parable of the dishonest manager – *Luke 16:1-14, p. 24.*

'In the beginning was the Word' – *John 1:1 p. 26.*

'Let there be light' – *Genesis 1:3, p. 26.*

Chapter 2

'It is not what goes into the mouth…' – *Matthew 15:11, pp. 33-49.*

'Blessed are you when people revile you' – *Matthew 5:11, p. 40.*

Adam and Eve eat the forbidden fruit – *Genesis 3, p. 43.*

'In the beginning was the Word' – *John 1:1 p. 43.*

'I am the living bread' – *John 6:51, p. 48.*

'Man shall not live by bread alone' – *Matthew 4:4, p. 48.*

'Take, eat; this is my body' – *Matthew 26:26, p. 48.*

Chapter 3

'You are the salt of the earth' – *Matthew 5: 13, pp. 58-77.*

Elijah purifies the water of a spring – *2 Kings 2:19-22, p. 59.*

'You shall not omit from your grain-offerings…' *Leviticus 2:13, p. 59.*

Chapter 4

'If the salt loses its flavour…' – *Matthew 5:13, pp. 81-92.*

210 - The Tree of the Knowledge of Good and Evil
Methods, not explanations, are the only valid answers to the problem of evil. Evil is an inner and outer reality which confronts us every day, and we must learn to deal with it.

211 - Freedom, the Spirit Triumphant
A human being is a spirit, a spark sprung from within the Almighty. Once a person understands, sees and feels this truth, he will be free.

212 - Light is a Living Spirit
Light, the living matter of the universe, is protection, nourishment and an agency for knowledge for human beings. Above all, it is the only truly effective means of self-transformation.

213 - Man's Two Natures, Human and Divine
Man is that ambiguous creature that evolution has placed on the borderline between the animal world and the divine world. His nature is ambivalent, and it is this ambivalence that he must understand and overcome.

214 - Hope for the World: Spiritual Galvanoplasty
On every level of the universe, the masculine and feminine principles reproduce the activity of those two great cosmic principles known as the Heavenly Father and the Divine Mother of which every manifestation of nature and life are a reflection. Spiritual galvanoplasty is a way of applying the science of these two fundamental principles to one's inner life.

215 - The True Meaning of Christ's Teaching
Jesus incorporated into the Our Father - or Lord's Prayer - an ancient body of knowledge handed down by Tradition and which had existed long before his time. A vast universe is revealed to one who knows how to interpret each of the requests formulated in this prayer.

216 - The Living Book of Nature
Everything in nature is alive and it is up to us to learn how to establish a conscious relationship with creation so as to receive that life within ourselves.

217 - New Light on the Gospels
The Parables and other tales from the Gospels are here interpreted as situations and events applicable to our own inner life.

218 - The Symbolic Language of Geometrical Figures
Each geometrical figure – circle, triangle, pentagram, pyramid or cross – is seen as a structure fundamental to the organization of the macrocosm (the universe) and the microcosm (human beings).

219 - Man's Subtle Bodies and Centres

However highly developed our sense organs, their scope will never reach beyond the physical plane. To experience richer and subtler sensations, human beings must exercise the subtler organs and spiritual centres that they also possess: the aura, the solar plexus, the Hara centre, the Chakras, and so on.

220 - The Zodiac, Key to Man and to the Universe

Those who are conscious of being part of the universe feel the need to work inwardly in order to find within themselves the fullness of the cosmic order so perfectly symbolized by the Zodiac.

221 - True Alchemy or The Quest for Perfection

Instead of fighting our weaknesses and vices – we would inevitably be defeated – we must learn to make them work for us. We think it normal to harness the untamed forces of nature, so why be surprised when a Master, an initiate, speaks of harnessing the primitive forces within us? This is true spiritual alchemy.

222 - Man's Psychic Life: Elements and Structures

"Know thyself." How to interpret this precept carved over the entrance to the temple at Delphi? To know oneself is to be conscious of one's different bodies, from the denser to the most subtle, of the principles which animate these bodies, of the needs they induce in one, and of the state of consciousness which corresponds to each.

223 - Creation: Artistic and Spiritual

Everyone needs to create but true creation involves spiritual elements. Artists, like those who seek the spirit, have to reach beyond themselves in order to receive elements from the higher planes.

224 - The Powers of Thought

Thought is a power, an instrument given to us by God so that we may become creators like himself – creators in beauty and perfection. This means that we must be extremely watchful, constantly verifying that what we do with our thoughts is truly for our own good and that of the whole world. This is the one thing that matters.

225 - Harmony and Health

Illness is a result of some physical or psychic disorder. The best defence against illness, therefore, is harmony. Day and night we must take care to be attuned and in harmony with life as a whole, with the boundless life of the cosmos.

226 - The Book of Divine Magic

True, divine magic, consists in never using the faculties, knowledge, or powers one has acquired for one's own self-interest, but always and only for the establishment of God's kingdom on earth.

227 - Golden Rules for Everyday Life

Why spoil one's life by chasing after things that matter less than life itself? Those who learn to give priority to life, who protect and preserve it in all integrity, will find more and more that they obtain their desires. For it is this, an enlightened, luminous life that can give them everything.

228 - Looking into the Invisible

Meditation, dreams, visions, astral projection all give us access to the invisible world, but the quality of the revelations received depends on our efforts to elevate and refine our perceptions.

229 - The Path of Silence

In every spiritual teaching, practices such as meditation and prayer have only one purpose: to lessen the importance attributed to one's lower nature and give one's divine nature more and more scope for expression. Only in this way can a human being experience true silence.

230 - The Book of Revelations: A Commentary

If *Revelations* is a difficult book to interpret it is because we try to identify the people, places and events it describes instead of concentrating on the essence of its message: a description of the elements and processes of our spiritual life in relation to the life of the cosmos.

231 - The Seeds of Happiness

Happiness is like a talent which has to be cultivated. Those who want to possess happiness must go in search of the elements which will enable them to nourish it inwardly; elements which belong to the divine world.

232 - The Mysteries of Fire and Water

Our psychic life is fashioned every day by the forces we allow to enter us, the influences that impregnate us. What could be more poetic, more meaningful than water and fire and the different forms under which they appear?

233 - Youth: Creators of the Future

Youth is full of life, enthusiasms and aspirations of every kind. The great question is how to channel its extraordinary, overflowing effervescence of energies.

234 - Truth, Fruit of Wisdom and Love

We all abide by our own "truth", and it is in the name of their personal "truth" that human beings are continually in conflict. Only those who possess true love and true wisdom discover the same truth and speak the same language.

235 - In Spirit and in Truth

Since we live on earth we are obliged to give material form to our religious beliefs. Sacred places and objects, rites, prayers and ceremonies are expressions of those beliefs. It is important to understand that they are no more than expressions – expressions which are always more or less inadequate. They are not themselves the religion, for religion exists in spirit and in truth.

236 - Angels and Other Mysteries of the Tree of Life

God is like a pure current of electricity which can reach us only through a series of transformers. These transformers are the countless luminous beings which inhabit the heavens and which tradition calls the Angelic Hierarchies. It is through them that we receive divine life; through them that we are in contact with God.

237 - Cosmic Balance, the Secret of Polarity

Libra – the Scales – symbolizes cosmic balance, the equilibrium of the two opposite and complementary forces, the masculine and feminine principles, by means of which the universe came into being and continues to exist. The symbolism of Libra, expression of this twofold polarity, dominates the whole of creation.

238 - The Faith That Moves Mountains

Faith is the result of an age-old knowledge buried deep within our subconscious. It is founded on an experience of the divine world, an experience which has left indelible traces on each one of us and which we must reanimate.

239 - Love Greater Than Faith

As long as we have not understood what true faith is, there can be no love; and conversely, as long as we do not know how to manifest love, we cannot claim that we have faith.

240 - Sons and Daughters of God

The love for one's neighbour which was taught by Jesus and which stems from this truth that humans are sons and daughters of the same Father has allowed the idea of brotherhood to forge a path.

241 - The Philosopher's Stone
in the Gospels and in Alchemy

The Gospels can be understood and interpreted in the light of alchemical science. On the face of it, they are simply giving an account of the life of one man, Jesus, born two thousand years ago in Palestine, but while they recount the different stages of his life, from birth to death and resurrection, they are in fact also describing alchemical processes.

World Wide - Editor-Distributor
Editions Prosveta S.A. - Z.A. Le Capitou - B.P. 12
F - 83601 Fréjus CEDEX (France)
Tel. (33) 04 94 19 33 33 – Fax (33) 04 94 19 33 34
Web: www.prosveta.com – e-mail: international@prosveta.com

Distributors

AUSTRALIA
PROSVETA Australia
P.O. Box 538 – Mittagong – N.S.W. 2575 Australia
Tel. (61) (0) 2 4855 0189 – Fax. (61) (0) 2 4872 2641
e-mail: prosveta.au@bigpond.com

AUSTRIA
HARMONIEQUELL VERSAND – Hof 37 – A- 5302 Henndorf am Wallersee
Tel. / fax (43) 6214 7413 – e-mail: info@prosveta.at

BELGIUM & LUXEMBOURG
PROSVETA BENELUX – Beeldenmakersstraat 1 – B 8000 Brugge
Tel./Fax. (32)(0)50/61 69 10 – e-mail: prosveta@skynet.be
N.V. MAKLU Somersstraat 13-15 – B-2000 Antwerpen
Tel. (32) 3/231 29 00 – Fax (32) 3/233 26 59
S.D.L. CARAVELLE S.A. – rue du Pré aux Oies, 303 – 1130 Bruxelles
Tel. (32) 2 240 93 00 – Fax (32) 2 216 35 98
e-mail: info@sdlcaravelle.com

BULGARIA
SVETOGLED – Bd Saborny 16 A, appt 11 – 9000 Varna
e-mail: vassil100@abv.bg – Tel/Fax: (359) 52 63 90 94

CANADA
PROSVETA Inc. – 3950, Albert Mines – Canton-de-Hatley (Qc), J0B 2C0
Tel. (819) 564-8212 – Fax. (819) 564-1823
in Canada, call toll free: 1-800-854-8212
e-mail: prosveta@prosveta-canada.com / www.prosveta-canada.com

CONGO
PROSVETA CONGO
29, Avenue de la Révolution – B.P. 768 – Pointe-Noire
Tel. : (242) 948156 / (242) 5531254 – Fax : (242) 948156
e-mail: prosvetacongo@yahoo.fr

COLOMBIA
ASOCIACIÓN PROSVETA
Calle 146 Número 13 - 10, Apart. 404 Interior 2 – Cedritos – Bogotá, Colombia
Tel. (57-1) 6 14 53 85 – Fax. (57-1) 6 33 58 03
Celular: (57) 311 8 10 25 42 – e-mail: kalagiya@hotmail.com

CYPRUS
THE SOLAR CIVILISATION BOOKSHOP – BOOKBINDING
73 D Kallipoleos Avenue – Lycavitos – P. O. Box 24947, 1355 – Nicosia
e-mail: cypapach@cytanet.com.cy – Tel / Fax 00357-22-377503

CZECH REPUBLIC
PROSVETA – Ant. Sovy 18 – České Budejovice 370 05
Tel / Fax: (420) 38-53 10 227 – e-mail: prosveta@iol.cz

FRANCE – DOM TOM
Editions Prosveta S.A. - B.P. 12 – F - 83601 Fréjus CEDEX (France)
Tel. (33) 04 94 19 33 33 – Fax (33) 04 94 19 33 34
e-mail: international@prosveta.com – www.prosveta.com

GERMANY
PROSVETA Verlag GmbH – Heerstrasse 55 – 78628 Rottweil
Tel. (49) 741-46551 – Fax. (49) 741-46552 – e-mail: prosveta7@aol.com

GREAT BRITAIN – IRELAND
PROSVETA – The Doves Nest, Duddleswell Uckfield – East Sussex TN 22 3JJ
Tel. (44) (01825) 712988 – Fax (44) (01825) 713386 – e-mail: prosveta@pavilion.co.uk

HAITI
PROSVETA DÉPÔT HAITI – Angle rue Faustin 1er et rue Bois Patate #25 bis
6110 Port-au-Prince
Tel. (509) 245 06 43 – Mobile: (509) 464 80 88 – e-mail: rbaaudant@yahoo.com

HOLLAND
STICHTING PROSVETA NEDERLAND
Zeestraat 50 – 2042 LC Zandvoort
Tel. (31) 33 25 345 75 – Fax. (31) 33 25 803 20 – e-mail: prosveta@worldonline.nl

ISRAEL
Zohar, P.B. 1046, Netanya 42110

ITALY
PROSVETA Coop. a r.l.
Casella Postale 55 – 06068 Tavernelle (PG)
Tel. (39) 075-835 84 98 – Fax (39) 075-835 97 12 – e-mail: prosveta@tin.it

IVORY COAST
Librairie Prosveta
25 rue Paul Langevin Zone 4C – 01 Abidjan
e-mail: prosvetafrique@yahoo.fr – Tel/Fax: (225) 21 25 42 11

LEBANON
PROSVETA LIBAN – P.O. Box 90-995
Jdeidet-el-Metn, Beirut – Tel. (03) 448560 – e-mail: prosveta_lb@terra.net.lb

NORWAY
PROSVETA NORDEN – Postboks 318, N-1502 Moss
Tel. (47) 69 26 51 40 – Fax (47) 69 26 51 08 – e-mail: info@prosveta.no

PORTUGAL
EDIÇÕES PROSVETA
Rua Palmira, 66 r/c - C – 1170 - 287 Lisboa
Tel. / Fax (351) 213 540 764 – e-mail: prosvetapt@hotmail.com

ROMANIA
ANTAR – Str. N. Constantinescu 10 – Bloc 16A - sc A - Apt. 9
Sector 1 – 71253 Bucarest
Tel. 004021-231 28 78 – Tel./ Fax 004021-231 37 19
e-mail : prosveta_ro@yahoo.com

RUSSIA
EDITIONS PROSVETA
143 964 Moskovskaya oblast, g. Reutov – 4, post/box 4
Tel./ Fax. (095) 525 18 17 – Tel. (095) 795 70 74 – e-mail: prosveta@online.ru

SPAIN
ASOCIACIÓN PROSVETA ESPAÑOLA – C/ Ausias March n° 23 Ático
SP-08010 Barcelona – Tel (34) (93) 412 31 85 – Fax (34) (93) 318 89 01
e-mail: aprosveta@prosveta.es

UNITED STATES
PROSVETA US Dist.
26450 Ruether Ave #205 – Santa Clarita CA 91350
Tel. (661) 251-5412 – Fax. (661) 252-1751
e-mail: prosveta-usa@earthlink.net. / www.prosveta-usa.com

SWITZERLAND
PROSVETA Société Coopérative
Ch. de la Céramone 2 – CH - 1808 Les Monts-de-Corsier
Tel. (41) 21 921 92 18 – Fax. (41) 21 922 92 04
e-mail: prosveta@bluewin.ch

VENEZUELA
PROSVETA VENEZUELA C. A. – Calle Madrid
Edificio La Trinidad – Las Mercedes – Caracas D.F.
Tel. (58) 414 134 75 34 – e-mail: prosvetavenezuela@gmail.com

Updated list 16.08.07. If you cannot contact one of these distributors,
consult the internet site www.prosveta.com

The aim of the Universal White Brotherhood association
is the study and practice of the Teaching
of Master Omraam Mikhaël Aïvanhov,
published and distributed
by Prosveta.

All enquiries about the association should be addressed to:
Universal White Brotherhood
The Doves Nest, Duddleswell, Uckfield
East Sussex TN22 3JJ, GREAT BRITAIN
Tel: (44) (0)1825 712150 – Fax: (44) (0)1825 713386
E-mail: uwb@pavilion.co.uk

───────────────────

Printed in October 2007
by DUMAS-TITOULET Imprimeurs
N° imprimeur : 45957- D
42004 Saint-Etienne – France

───────────

Dépôt légal: octobre 2007